Network Automation Using Python 3

An Administrator's Handbook

EDITION 2, 2020

Jithin Aby Alex

About the Author

Jithin Aby Alex, CISSP, CEH

Security Professional, having experience in managing security operations, implementing and handling major security solutions and products in various environments and regions. I have used my experience, professional connections and publicly available information for writing this book. Personally, I thank you for purchasing this book and thanks for the support. I hope this book will be informative to you and I wish you all the best.

Please visit www.jaacostan.com for my articles and technical write-ups.

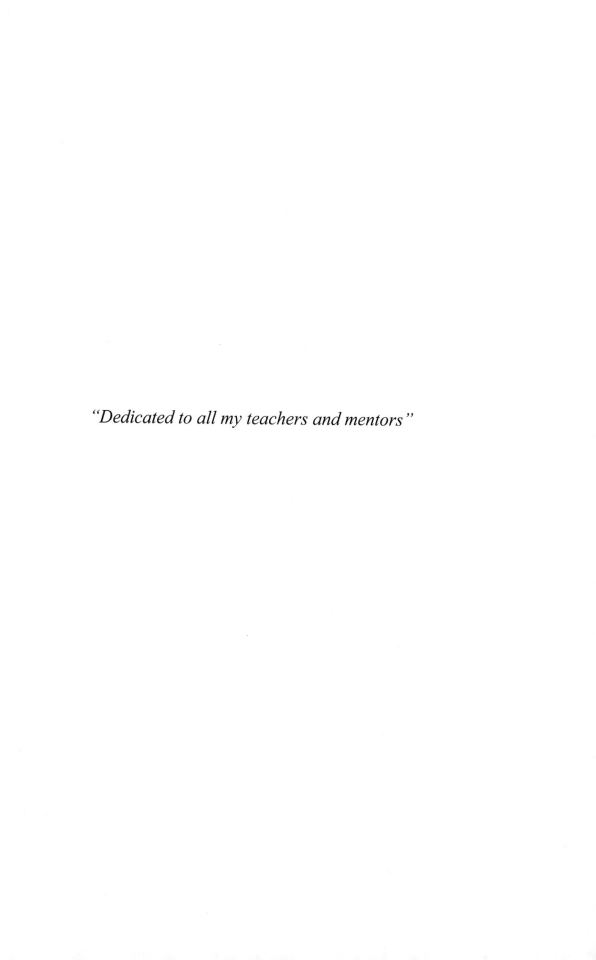

"Dedicated to all my teachers and mentors"

Table of Contents

1.1 What is Network Automation?

Network automation is the process of automating the configuration, management and operations of a computer network. The tasks that were normally done by the network or system administrator can be automated using a number of tools and technologies. As we know, human errors is the number one reason for most of the issues including unavailability, downtime, security etc. in a network environment. A proper automation will eliminate the human errors and also speed up the operations, thus saving time and cost. Network automation is implemented through the combination of hardware and software-based solutions that automatically execute repetitive tasks in a network environment.

Scripting languages are widely used by Network and System administrators for automating the tasks. This saves time, effort and thereby reducing human errors as well. Among the Network Automation tools, Python and Ansible are the most popular ones. With Software Defined Networking (SDN) in picture, knowing any of these programming languages is vital for the future of administering the network and systems.

1.2 How the book is written?

This Second edition book is written in a structured manner. First get familiarize with the basics of python3 such as data types, lists, conditions, loops, libraries etc. Every concept is explained with examples.

Once you get familiarized with the basics and concepts, let's get in to the real world applications of python3 in network administration. I have included many useful and practical examples that you might encounter in you daily administering tasks. Such as, changing configurations of multiple network devices, taking backup of multiple devices etc. in a single go using python3 script.

Feel free to revise the topics whenever you feel lost. Everything is written in simple language and I recommend you to practice each examples and exercises multiple times until you really understood the topics and concepts. I also encourage you to try writing the codes yourself. Practice keeps you in a better place. I wish you all the best. Let's get started.

1.3 Pre-requisites.

I assume those who are reading this book have a prior knowledge on IT networking especially with Cisco IOS. There is no programming experience required for practicing the concepts referred in this book and for that reason, I have tried to explain all concepts from the basics itself.

Kindly note, don't consider this book as a core python developer guide. This book is primarily intended for networking professionals on how to make use of python programming to automate their network administration tasks.

If you want to do a deep dive on just the Python3 programming language, I recommend you to read the book "Learn Python3 the hard way." https://learnpythonthehardway.org/python3/

Next, for practicing the network automation, either you should have some real network devices such as switches and routers, or you can practice it in GNS3 simulation software. In this book, I have explained the practical's using GNS3 virtual lab. So from required software aspect, GNS3 and latest version of Python3 are the prerequisites.

1.4 Why Python?

One of the popular high level and easiest programming language which is used everywhere including software applications, the Web, operating systems etc. Also the resources related to python is available widely over the internet.

- Easy to install
- Readable and easy to understand

- Large community support.

The most widely implemented version of python is Python2. But Python3 is getting popular now and at present, most of the new applications and programs are written in Python3.

While writing the code, there is no big difference in Python3 compared to Python2. But, with future in mind, it is better to write the codes in python3.

1.5 How to Install Python 3?

In Linux python is usually comes preinstalled. For Windows OS, you can download python from the internet and install.

1) Install Python 3

Download python from the Python website. **https://www.python.org/downloads/**

Python >>> Downloads >>> Windows

Python Releases for Windows

- Latest Python 3 Release - Python 3.7.0
- Latest Python 2 Release - Python 2.7.15

- Python 3.7.0 - 2018-06-27
  - Download Windows x86 web-based installer

To know more on how to install python on your machine, visit **https://docs.python.org/3/using/windows.html**

2) Verify the python is running in your machine.

Go to command prompt or shell, and type python. It will show the version installed.

```
C:\Users\Jaa>python
Python 3.6.4 (v3.6.4:d48eceb, Dec 19 2017, 06:54:40) [MSC v.1900 64 bit (AMD64)] on win32
Type "help", "copyright", "credits" or "license" for more information.
>>>
```

Use quit() or Ctrl-Z plus Return to exit

1.5.1 Setup path and environment variable

Once Python is successfully installed, specify environment variables if you want to execute python scrips from a specific path. This step is completely optional if you decide to execute the scripts from the python root directory only.

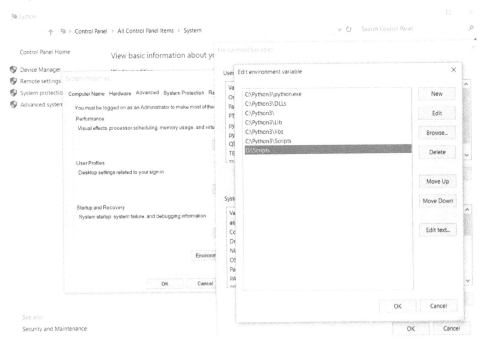

Go to your system properties either from control panel or by right clicking **My Computer** and **properties**.

Click on **Advanced System Settings -> Advanced -> Environment Variables -> select python3** and click **edit**, and add a **new** path.

Here in this illustration, I have added a new path **D:\Scripts**. Which means I can execute the scripts in the folder directly using python3. You can specify the folder of your wish.

1.5.2 Important things to consider in python:

1) Indentation matters.

Unlike other programming languages, Python considers Indentations and those spaces are very important. Improper indentation leads to error. Python usually follows a 4 spaces indentation. I will be explaining about this in the coming chapters.

```
for i in range(10)
    print(i)
```

Other Programming languages uses curly brackets {} for showing the code blocks, while python uses Indentation.

import this command gives us a broad overview of Python3 in an easy readable way.

```
D:\Scripts>python
Python 3.6.4 (v3.6.4:d48eceb, Dec 19 2017, 06:54:40) [MSC v.1900 64 bit (AMD64)] on win32
Type "help", "copyright", "credits" or "license" for more information.
>>> import this
The Zen of Python, by Tim Peters

Beautiful is better than ugly.
Explicit is better than implicit.
Simple is better than complex.
Complex is better than complicated.
Flat is better than nested.
Sparse is better than dense.
Readability counts.
Special cases aren't special enough to break the rules.
Although practicality beats purity.
Errors should never pass silently.
Unless explicitly silenced.
In the face of ambiguity, refuse the temptation to guess.
There should be one-- and preferably only one --obvious way to do it.
Although that way may not be obvious at first unless you're Dutch.
Now is better than never.
Although never is often better than *right* now.
If the implementation is hard to explain, it's a bad idea.
If the implementation is easy to explain, it may be a good idea.
Namespaces are one honking great idea -- let's do more of those!
>>>
```

2) While declaring variable name, you can use alpha-numeric characters and underscore _.

Other characters are not allowed in a variable. Also note that, you cannot begin a variable name with an underscore character. Also you are not allowed to create a variable name that begins with a number.

Eg: **my_name** is a valid variable

my-name is not a valid variable because it used the hyphen character.

22name is not a valid variable because it begins with a number.

name_22 is a valid variable.

3) You can use either single quotes (') or double quotes (")

If you begins with single quote then close it with the same single quote. As a best practice, don't mix up single and double quotes in your code.

```
my_ip1 = '1.1.1.1'
my_ip2 = "1.1.1.1"
```

You can directly run commands on the python interpreter shell and can get output instantly.

```
>>> my_ip = '1.2.3.4'
>>> my_ip
'1.2.3.4'
>>>
```

See the data type using "type" command.

```
>>> my_ip = '1.2.3.4'
>>> my_ip
'1.2.3.4'
>>> type(my_ip)
<class 'str'>
>>>
```

The variable **my_ip** is declared as a '**str**' or String.

So, as with every programming lectures, let's begin with a simple **Hello world** program.

Open a test editor like notepad or notepad++ and write the following.

```
my_string = 'Hello World'
print(my_string)
```

```
my_string = 'Hello World'
print(my_string)
```

Save this as a .py file. In my example I saved it as **test.py**

Run this file in the interpreter shell to see the output.

Remember, I have set the path **D:\Scripts** in the environment variables, so that I can run the scripts contained in this folder directly with python.

```
Microsoft Windows [Version 10.0.17134.285]
(c) 2018 Microsoft Corporation. All rights reserved.

C:\Users\Jaa>D:

D:\>cd Scripts

D:\Scripts>test.py
Hello World

D:\Scripts>
```

When it comes to professional use, people use different IDEs instead of using the python interpreter shell for writing and executing the python scripts. I use IntelliJ Idea and PyCharm from JetBrains. But you can use any IDEs of your wish and convenience. Our intention is just to execute the scripts properly. The outputs shown here after is captured from IntelliJ IDEA.

Download PyCharm: https://www.jetbrains.com/pycharm/download/

What is an IDE?

An integrated development environment (IDE) is a software application that provides comprehensive facilities to computer programmers for code development. An IDE normally consists of a source code editor, build automation tools, and a debugger. Also provides code completion. You can still write code in a traditional way. Like, write the code in a text editor and save it as a .py file. Then call and execute the file in Python Interpreter shell. An IDE is used for a better GUI, debugging and code completion options.

Also if you are using windows, for running Netmiko (I will explain about Netmiko in detail in the following chapters), you may need to install Anaconda application. Anaconda itself has a python IDE package called as Spyder. It is optional, since we are discussing about IDE's, I just added it here as a note.

A note of Python3 backward compatibility

To offer backward compatibility with Python 2 from your Python 3 code, you can use the following commands at the top of each .py script.

```
from __future__ import absolute_import
from __future__ import division
from __future__ import print_function
from __future__ import unicode_literals
```

This is just for your information. This book focuses on Python3 and hence backward compatibility is not discussed here after.

2 Understand the Basics

Since this book is written for Network administrators to become familiar with python and how to use it in your daily operational tasks, I won't be going in to in depth basics of python programming. But still, you as an administrator should gain some amount of knowledge of the python programming. Remember, each commands I specify here has a lot of sub commands and associated options.

2.1 Standard Input and Output Operation

`input` command is used in python to capture the user input. In this example, the user is prompted to enter his IP address and the value is stored directly to variable named as `ip_add`.

```
ip_add = input("Enter your IP address : ")
print(ip_add)
```

```
stdinput.py
    ip_add = input("Enter your IP address : ")
    print(ip_add)

Run:    stdinput
    C:\Users\Jaa\AppData\Local\Programs\Python\Python36\python.exe D:/Workbook/Python/Network/stdinput.py
    Enter your IP address : 1.1.1.1
    1.1.1.1

    Process finished with exit code 0
```

When the script is executed, it will prompt the user to enter your IP address. Once user enters, then it will be shown as output.

2.2 Python Strings

By default he python3 stores the strings in a Unicode format. Prior to Python3, it was using ASCII as default which is only 8 bytes in length. To accommodate more languages and characters, Python3 adopts Unicode representations for all strings by default.

If you want to change the Unicode to ASCII in Python3, then prefix the string with a "**b**". This is shown below.

```
>>> my_ip = '1.1.1.1'
>>> type(my_ip)
<class 'str'>
>>> my_ip = b'1.1.1.1'
>>> type(my_ip)
<class 'bytes'>
>>>
```

We will be using this in the following exercises. With examples, you will be able to understand much better.

Comparison Operators

Equals	==
Not Equals	!=
Greater Than	>, >=
Less Than	<, <=
Assignment	=

Equals (==) is a checking operator. I illustrated it below. First I assign an IP address 1.1.1.1 to the variable ip_add. Then I used the Equals operator to check the weather value of the variable ip_add is 2.2.2.2. Python returned a response "False". Which means the variable value is not true. Next I used the Not Equals (!=) operator. Is the variable value is not equal to 2.2.2.2? The python responds as True.

```
>>> ip_add = '1.1.1.1'
>>> ip_add == '2.2.2.2'
False
>>> ip_add != '2.2.2.2'
True
>>> ip_add >= '2.2.2.2'
False
>>> ip_add <= '2.2.2.2'
True
>>>
```

Similarly I checked the other comparison operators Greater than and Less than to check the values of the Variable. These comparison operators are useful while writing the code. For example, if you want to find the active IP address in the network which is greater than 192.168.20.40. We can make use of these operators while writing the code.

We can also use the comparison operators in a different way.

For example, if you want to check 1.1 is a part of ip_add, then,

```
>>> '1.1' in ip_add
True
>>> '3.4' in ip_add
False
>>>
```

Each strings are stored with indices.

IP address	1	.	1	.	1	.	1
Indices	0	1	2	3	4	5	6

If I want to see the particular value of a position (indices) for the above IP address 1.1.1.1,

```
>>> ip_add[0]
'1'
>>> ip_add[2]
'1'
>>> ip_add[3]
'.'
>>>
```

String Concatenation

When we want to join two strings together, use + operator.

```
>>> my_string = 'My IP Address: '
>>> my_ip = '192.168.1.1'
>>> my_data = my_string + my_ip
>>> my_data
'My IP Address: 192.168.1.1'
>>>
```

Space and New Line Options

- /n is used for new line

- /t is used for an extra space

Use of Triple Quotes ('''') or ("""")

When you want to write a string value in multiple lines, then make use of triple quotes.

Begins with triple quote and ends with triple quotes as well.

```
my_str = '''hi hello
how are you
where are you'''
print(my_str)
```

```
stdinput ×
    C:\Users\Jaa\AppData\Local\Programs\Python\Pyth
    hi hello
    how are you
    where are you

    Process finished with exit code 0
```

In the native python interpreter shell, you may see the output as below. It shows the python internal representation as the output. You can clearly see the **\n** that represents a new line.

```
>>> my_string = ''' hello how are you
... i am good and
... what about you '''
>>> my_string
' hello how are you\ni am good and\nwhat about you '
>>>
```

Sometimes, the new line causes mistakes in formatting. See the example below.

```
my_dir = 'D:\netowrk\scripts\test\python'
print(my_dir)
```

```
stdinput ×
C:\Users\Jaa\AppData\Local\Programs\Python\Python36\python.exe
D:
etowrk\scripts  est\python

Process finished with exit code 0
```

I have specified my directory path by python mistakenly interpreted /n of /network as new line and you can see that in the above picture.

In order to avoid this, while specifying sting like this, prefix an "r" in the string. "r" tells python that this string is a raw string. Now you can see the output as you desired.

```
my_dir = r'D:\network\scripts\test\python'
print(my_dir)
```

```
stdinput ×
C:\Users\Jaa\AppData\Local\Programs\Python\Python36\pyth
D:\network\scripts\test\python

Process finished with exit code 0
```

Strip Command

To remove whitespaces, use strip command.

Consider the following string. It does have a lot of whitespace character in it.

```
my_string = '   hi,how are you?    '
```

```
>>> my_string = '   hi,how are you?   '
>>> my_string.strip()
'hi,how are you?'
>>> my_string.lstrip()
'hi,how are you?   '
>>> my_string.rstrip()
'   hi,how are you?'
>>>
```

`my_string.strip()` to strip off all the whitespaces

`my_string_lstrip()` to strip the whitespaces on the left

`my_string.rstrip()` to strip the whitespaces on the right

Split Command

Split command is used to split a string based on a particular character.

E.g.: `ip_add = '192.168.1.2'`

Split this IP Address based on character "."

`ip_add.split(".")` and output is shown as a python list.

```
>>> ip_add = '192.168.1.2'
>>> ip_add.split('.')
['192', '168', '1', '2']
>>>
```

I will be discussing more about Python List in the coming chapters.

If you have a string with multiple lines and you want to split the paragraph line by line, the use "\n" as the delimiter.

```
>>> my_str = '''hi, hello
... how are you
... where are you
... see you later'''
>>> my_str.split('\n')
['hi, hello', 'how are you', 'where are you', 'see you later']
>>>
```

2.3 Formatting the Output.

In this section, I am explaining different methods to format the input and outputs. Just get familiar with these. Formatting the code is helpful for easy reading and for reducing the code size. I will discuss some of the important formatting methods.

1) If you want to print a character to a number of times, then use the multiplication (star character *).

```
>>> my_char = '-hello-' * 20
>>> my_char
'-hello--hello--hello--hello--hello--hello--hello--hello--hello--hello--
hello--hello--hello--hello--hello--hello--hello--hello--hello--hello-'
>>>
```

2) Using the format command.

Call the value using format command. Populate the variable values at the desired positions. Also can be called them as named arguments.

```
>>> ip1 = '1.1.1.1'
>>> ip2 = '2.2.2.2'
>>> ip3 = '3.3.3.3'
>>> print('{} {} {}'.format(ip1, ip2, ip3))
1.1.1.1 2.2.2.2 3.3.3.3
```

You can specify the width inside the brackets {} as well.

```
>>> print('{} {} {}'.format(ip1, ip2, ip3))
1.1.1.1 2.2.2.2 3.3.3.3
>>> print('{:20} {:20} {:20}'.format(ip1, ip2, ip3))
1.1.1.1              2.2.2.2              3.3.3.3
>>>
```

To align the string to the right use {:>} and for left, use {:>} and for center align, use {:^}.

```
>>> print('{:>20} {:>20} {:>20}'.format(ip1, ip2, ip3))
             1.1.1.1              2.2.2.2              3.3.3.3
>>> print('{:<20} {:<20} {:<20}'.format(ip1, ip2, ip3))
1.1.1.1              2.2.2.2              3.3.3.3
>>>
```

To call the named arguments, specify the name in the statement as well. Eg:
Sam=ip1

```
>>>
>>>
>>> print('{Sam:<20} {Lisa:<20} {Peter:<20}'.format(Sam=ip1, Lisa=ip2, Peter=ip3))
1.1.1.1              2.2.2.2              3.3.3.3
>>>
>>>
```

3) Usage of "f" String

To call the variables directly in a print statement, use "f" string.

```
>>>
>>> print(f"Sam'sIP :{ip1} Lisa's IP :{ip2} Peter's IP :{ip3}")
Sam'sIP :1.1.1.1 Lisa's IP :2.2.2.2 Peter's IP :3.3.3.3
>>>
>>>
```

If you are finding little hard to understand the concepts, don't worry and note that these are some of the basic concepts to write the codes efficiently. Just try to write these codes and practice yourself, I assure you that, with practice you will understand the concepts fast, easy and better.

2.4 Dealing with Numbers

Arithmetic operations are pretty simple and straight forward in Python3.

Addition	+
Division /	/
Subtraction	-
Multiplication	*

In python3, when it comes to division, it automatically considers the variables as float values.

Though the variables were integers, when the division is performed, python provides the output as float.

```
>>> num1 = 5
>>> num2 = 2
>>> type(num1)
<class 'int'>
>>> type(num2)
<class 'int'>
>>> num1 / num2
2.5
>>> num3 = num1 / num2
>>> type(num3)
<class 'float'>
>>>
```

To convert a float to integer or vice-versa,

```
>>> num3
2.5
>>> int(num3)
2
>>> float(num3)
2.5
>>>
```

Rounding a float value using round command.

Assume you have a float value 5.827298 and you want to round it up to two points or round the value as whole, use the round command.

```
>>> num4 = 5.827298
>>> round(num4, 2)
5.83
>>>
>>> round(num4)
6
>>>
```

To convert a variable value to Hex/Decimal/Binary. I have illustrated the example below.

I have a port number 8080 and I want to convert the port number value to Hexa-decimal or Binary.

```
>>> port1 = 8080
>>> hex(port1)
'0x1f90'
>>>
>>> bin(port1)
'0b1111110010000'
```

2.5 Reading Input from Files

Reading the contents of a file. It take place in the following sequence.

Load the file, read and then show as the output, finally close the file.

```
my_file = open('D:\Scripts\ios_startup.txt')
data = my_file.read()
print(data)
```

1) Open the file.

```
my_file = open('D:\Scripts\ios_startup.txt')
```

In this illustration, my sample file is "ios_startup.txt" and is located at location "D:\Scripts\". I load the file in to a named variable my_file (This can be any name).

2) Read the contents of the file.

Read the contents of the file using read command. I saved the contents of the file to the variable named "data"

```
data = my_file.read()
```

3) Output the contents.

```
my_file = open('D:\Scripts\ios_startup.txt')
data = my_file.read()
print(data)


fineinput ×
C:\Users\Jaa\AppData\Local\Programs\Python\Python36\python.exe
!
service timestamps debug datetime msec
service timestamps log datetime msec
no service password-encryption
!
hostname %h
!
ip cef
no ip domain-lookup
no ip icmp rate-limit unreachable
ip tcp synwait 5
no cdp log mismatch duplex
!
line con 0
 exec-timeout 0 0
 logging synchronous
```

There is another way if you want to print the output directly rather than declaring and loading the data in to another variable.

```
my_file = open('D:\Scripts\ios_startup.txt')
print(my_file.read())
```

```
fineinput ×
    !
    service timestamps debug datetime msec
    service timestamps log datetime msec
    no service password-encryption
    !
    hostname %h
    !
    ip cef
    no ip domain-lookup
    no ip icmp rate-limit unreachable
```

4) Close the operation using close command.

my_file.close() is used to close the operation.

```
my_file = open('D:\Scripts\ios_startup.txt')
data = my_file.read()
print(data)
my_file.close()
```

Reading Line by Line

If you need to read the contents of the file line by line, then use readline command.

For illustration purpose of this readline operation, I used the native python interpreter shell.

```
>>> f = open('D:\Scripts\ios_startup.txt')
>>> f.readline()
'!\n'
>>> f.readline()
'service timestamps debug datetime msec\n'
>>> f.readline()
'service timestamps log datetime msec\n'
>>> f.readline()
'no service password-encryption\n'
>>> f.readline()
'!\n'
>>> f.readline()
'hostname %h\n'
>>>
```

I load the file to a variable f and use the readline() operation. You can see the output line by line. After displaying each line, the user need to press enter for the next line.

2.6 Lists

Grouping sequential data or elements can be called as a python list. We can have different data types included together in a list

Creating a list

```
new_list = []
```

```
Eg: sample_list = ['IP Address', 80, 44.20]
```

```
>>> sample_list = ['IP Address', 80 , 44.20]
>>> sample_list
['IP Address', 80, 44.2]
>>>
```

To append data in to an existing list,

```
sample_list.append('port number')
```

```
>>> sample_list.append('Port Number')
>>> sample_list
['IP Address', 80, 44.2, 'Port Number']
>>>
```

To count the number of occurrences

```
sample_list.count('80')
```

```
>>> sample_list
['IP Address', 80, 44.2, 'Port Number']
>>> sample_list.count(80)
1
>>>
```

Remove: Use pop method by Specifying the index or use remove command and specify the value.

```
sample_list.pop(0)
```

```
>>> sample_list
['IP Address', 80, 44.2, 'Port Number']
>>> sample_list.pop(0)
'IP Address'
>>> sample_list
[80, 44.2, 'Port Number']
>>>
```

```
sample_list.remove('44.20')
```

```
>>> sample_list
[80, 44.2, 'Port Number']
>>> sample_list.remove(44.2)
>>> sample_list
[80, 'Port Number']
>>>
```

We can create a list from a file. Like grab the first 5 lines of in a file and save it as a python list.

```
f = open('ios_startup.txt')
data = f.readlines()
data[0:4]
```

Or get data from lines number 8 to 12

```
data[7:11]
```

```
>>> f = open('D:\Scripts\ios_startup.txt')
>>> output = f.readlines()
>>> output[0:4]
['!\n', 'service timestamps debug datetime msec\n', 'service timestamps log d
atetime msec\n', 'no service password-encryption\n']
>>> output[7:11]
['ip cef\n', 'no ip domain-lookup\n', 'no ip icmp rate-limit unreachable\n',
'ip tcp synwait 5\n']
>>>
```

Join Operation

If you want to join an already split string, then you may use the join operation.

```
>>> my_ip = '192.168.10.20'
>>> my_ip.split('.')
['192', '168', '10', '20']
>>> ip = my_ip.split('.')
>>> ip
['192', '168', '10', '20']
>>> '.'.join(ip)
'192.168.10.20'
>>> ip
['192', '168', '10', '20']
>>> '#'.join(ip)
'192#168#10#20'
>>>
```

In the above example, I split an IP address and save the output on a variable named as "ip".

Then I used the join operator to join the list with the character I want. Here I used "." and "#" characters as examples.

2.7 Dictionaries

Dictionaries are used to map key value pairs. They are used when the data is not in a sequence and has miscellaneous information. We will be using this during the SSH management of switches.

Declare a dictionary named as **switch.**

```
switch = {'cisco': '4500',
    'ip': '1.1.1.1',
    'location': 'Perth'}
```

```
>>>
>>>
>>> switch = {'cisco': '4500',
... 'ip address': '1.1.1.1',
... 'location': 'Perth',
... }
>>> switch
{'cisco': '4500', 'ip address': '1.1.1.1', 'location': 'Perth'}
>>>
```

To add a key in to the existing dictionary, you can use the following command.

```
switch['serial number'] = 'ABCD1234'
```

```
>>> switch
{'cisco': '4500', 'ip address': '1.1.1.1', 'location': 'Perth'}
>>>
>>> switch['serial number'] = 'ABCD1234'
>>> switch
{'cisco': '4500', 'ip address': '1.1.1.1', 'location': 'Perth', 'serial number': 'ABCD1234'}
>>>
```

2.8 Conditions

If statement

If loop works like, if the particular statement is true, then do the following else do this.

In the following condition, I declare a variable value1 with a value 20. Condition check: if the value is 20, then print the value as 20 else print value is not 20.

```
>>> if value1 == 20:
...    print("value is 20")
... else:
...    print("value 1 is not 20")
...
value is 20
```

Elif condition.

Else-If conditions are used when you have multiple conditions to check inside an IF statement.

```
>>> value1 = 20
>>> if value1 == 10:
...     print("value is 10")
... elif value1 == 30:
...     print("value is 30")
... else:
...     print("value is 20")
...
value is 20
>>>
```

Example:

```
value1 = input("Enter a value.10 or 20 or 30 :")
if value1 == '10':
    print("value is 10")
elif value1 == '20':
    print("value is 20")
else:
    print("value is 30")
```

```
elif value1 == '20'
```

```
 if statement ×
    C:\Users\Jaa\AppData\Local\Programs\Python\Python36\python.exe
    Enter a value.10 or 20 or 30 :10
    value is 10

    Process finished with exit code 0
```

In the above code, prompt the user to enter a value 10, 20 or 30.

1) If the value is 10, print the output values as 10

2) Else if the value is 20, then print the output value as 20

3) Else any other value than 10 or 20, show the output value as 30.

Note that, the data type of the variable value1 is string. That's why I put a quotes in the "if" statements, if value1 == **'10'.**

You can write the code like this as well. Get the string input from the user and then convert the string value to integer, then perform the condition check.

```
value1 = input("Enter a value.10 or 20 or 30 :")
value1 = int(value1) # String value is converted to Integer here
if value1 == 10:
    print("value is 10")
elif value1 == 20:
    print("value is 20")
else:
    print("value is 30")
```

```
if statement ×
C:\Users\Jaa\AppData\Local\Programs\Python\Python36\python.exe "D:/W
Enter a value.10 or 20 or 30 :10
value is 10

Process finished with exit code 0
```

Note: Always try different logics while writing your code. Those practicing makes your programming and knowledge better.

```
elif value1 == 20:
⇒print("value is 20")
else:
⇒print("value is 30")
```

Note: Always keep the indentations. This is very important in python. Normally a 4 whitespace indentation is applied in the python programming.

2.9 Loops

Loops are checking a sequence of conditions and Continue running the block of code until the condition satisfies.

For Loop.

For each time though the loop, it check for each values in the list one by one until the condition finishes.

```
my_list = [1, 2, 3, 4]
for i in my_list:
    print("value is ", i)
print("loop finished")
```

```
for loop ×
   C:\Users\Jaa\AppData\Local\Programs\Python\Python36\py
   value is  1
   value is  2
   value is  3
   value is  4
   loop finished

   Process finished with exit code 0
```

In the above example, I created a simple list with 4 values 1,2,3,4.

In the **for loop**, the condition **"i"** will check each values in the list **my_list** and when the list finished or run out, it execute the final statement.

If I explain the above for loop in simple terms,

1) **my_list** is a simple list with 4 values **1,2,3,4.**

2) Now the for loop executes,

3) The variable named as **"i"** check for each values from **my_list**

4) **"i"** loads the first value from the list and print the output

5) **"i"** loads the second value from the list and print the output

6) **"i"** loads the third value from the list and print the output

7) **"i"** loads the fourth value from the list and print the output

8) There are no more numbers available in the list and hence the loop is finished and executes the final statement "loop finished".

Example:

Check each IP address in the list and print the output.

```
ip_list = ['192.168.1.1', '192.168.20.30', '10.10.10.30']
for ip in ip_list:
    print("IP is", ip)
```

```
for loop ×
C:\Users\Jaa\AppData\Local\Programs\Python\Python36\python.exe "
IP is 192.168.1.1
IP is 192.168.20.30
IP is 10.10.10.30
```

Another example,

Print number 0 to 9 using **for loop.**

```
for i in range(10):
    print(i)
```

```
ping 1to10 ×
C:\Users\Jaa\AppData\Local\Programs\Python
0
1
2
3
4
5
6
7
8
9

Process finished with exit code 0
```

In this example, we also used the range statement, where the **i** value will check the range which we specified. Here in this example, the range is 10. So it increment one starting from 0 until 9.

Break statement.

If we need to break the **for loop,** include break statements in the loop.

```
ip_list = ['192.168.1.1', '192.168.20.30', '10.10.10.30']
for ip in ip_list:
    print("IP is", ip)
    if ip == '192.168.20.30':
        break
```

```
for ip in ip_list  >  if ip == '192.168.20.30'
for loop  ×
    C:\Users\Jaa\AppData\Local\Programs\Python\Python36\python.exe
    IP is 192.168.1.1
    IP is 192.168.20.30

    Process finished with exit code 0
```

In the above example, the break statement is included in such a way that, if the variable **ip** encounter the IP address value **192.168.20.30** in the list, then break the loop operation.

You can see the **for loop** operation stops when the **if statement** satisfies, and the last IP in the list is not checked in this loop.

Continue Statement

Continue statement is used when the particular if statement is matched, then instead of continuing the next statement, it continue with the loop statement.

In the example shown below, when the **if statement** is matched, which means when **ip** value is matched to 192.168.20.30, then instead of continuing with the print statement it continues with the **for loop.** So in the output, you can see all the IP values except 192.168.20.30. With continue statement, the **for loop** is not breaking at any point of time.

```
ip_list = ['192.168.1.1', '192.168.20.30', '10.10.10.30']
for ip in ip_list:
    if ip == '192.168.20.30':
        continue
    print("IP is", ip)
```

```
for ip in ip_list    if ip == '192.168.20.30'

for loop ×

C:\Users\Jaa\AppData\Local\Programs\Python\Python36\python.exe
IP is 192.168.1.1
IP is 10.10.10.30

Process finished with exit code 0
```

While loop

If the given expression is true, then the code block under the while loop will be executed. The loop will be exit when the while expression is not more true.

In the example below, I declare a variable **i** with initial value as 0.

Then in the while loop is constructed, until the value of **i** is less than or equal to 5, execute the while loop. During each instance print the current value of **i**, then increment the value of I with1. When the value of **i** reached 5, then while loop condition is not more true and it get exit.

```
i = 0
while i <= 5:
    print('the current value is ', i)
    i = i + 1
print('loop finished')
```

```
whileloop ×

C:\Users\Jaa\AppData\Local\Programs\Python\Python36\p
the current value is  0
the current value is  1
the current value is  2
the current value is  3
the current value is  4
the current value is  5
loop finished

Process finished with exit code 0
```

2.10 Python Functions

What would you do, when you need light in your room? We just buy a bulb and use it, right? Exactly. We don't need to know how a bulb is manufactured and what are the components used inside a bulb. All we need to know is why and where to use it.

Functions are similar to the above concept. Functions are a code block or a section in the program that is used to perform a specific task. Once you have a function in your code, you can used it multiple times, where ever you want in your code.

The only time you need to know how a function works inside is when you need to write the function or to change how it work or to tweak the functionality.

There are many predefined functions in pythons which are developed by various developers in the community to perform certain tasks. We may use it during the lab exercises in the coming chapters.

To define a function in python,

`def hello_world():` //hello_world is the new function name

> `print("This is a Hello World Function")`

`hello_world()` // Calling the function here

```
def hello_world():
    print("This is a Hello World Function")


hello_world()
```

```
python functions ×
C:\Users\Jaa\AppData\Local\Programs\Python\Python36\python.exe
This is a Hello World Function

Process finished with exit code 0
```

Passing argument values in a function.

Normally functions does some serious operations in a program. For example, I have created a calculator function code.

First I defined a function named as calc with two arguments inside v1 and v2.

```
def calc(v1, v2)
```

Inside the calc function, the code will perform the four mathematical operations such as addition, Multiplication, division and subtraction. So whatever the value passed by the function arguments v1 and v2 will be used for the mathematical functions.

So now the function named as **calc(v1, v2)** has been created, with two arguments inside.

Now I declared two variables **a** and **b**, and prompt the input numbers from the user. The values are further passed in to the function, then function performs the calculations and shows the output.

```
calc(int(a), int(b))
```

```
def calc(v1, v2):
    print('addition          :', v1 + v2)
    print('multiplication    :', v1 * v2)
    print('division          :', v1 / v2)
    print('subtraction       :', v1 - v2)
    return


a = input('Enter the first number    :')
b = input('Enter the Second number   :')
calc(int(a), int(b))
```

```
calc()
python fn calc ×
C:\Users\Jaa\AppData\Local\Programs\Python\Python36\python.exe
Enter the first number    :10
Enter the Second number   :5
addition         : 15
multiplication   : 50
division         : 2.0
subtraction      : 5

Process finished with exit code 0
```

Note that since the operations are mathematical, I converted the values **a** and **b** to integers, otherwise the code will return error. The value **a** is passed inside the function equivalent to **v1** and **b** equivalent to **v2**.

All the variables defined inside a function is locally significant. The same variable name defined outside the function is different than the one inside the function.

I have illustrated this in the following picture. Though there are two variables names ad v1 and v2 inside function, I used the same names and declared v1 and v2 outside the functions with values 555 and 666 respectively. These values are not used by the function.

```
def calc(v1, v2):
    print('addition            :', v1 + v2)
    print('multiplication      :', v1 * v2)
    print('division            :', v1 / v2)
    print('subtraction         :', v1 - v2)
    return


v1 = 555
v2 = 666
a = input('Enter the first number    :')
b = input('Enter the Second number   :')
calc(int(a), int(b))
```

```
python fn calc ×
C:\Users\Jaa\AppData\Local\Programs\Python\Python36\python.ex
Enter the first number    : 8
Enter the Second number   : 4
addition            : 12
multiplication      : 32
division            : 2.0
subtraction         : 4

Process finished with exit code 0
```

Section Summary

In this section, we discussed the fundamental basic building blocks of python programming such as data types, formats, lists, conditionals and loops, functions etc. You should be very clear about these basics and you may use it while writing the codes yourselves.

In the next section, we will be learning, practicing and writing some of the real-world application examples in network automation using the python3 programming. Let's get started.

3 Exercises

In this section, we will be writing python codes, executing it in a lab environment, analyze and understand the changes. But before jumping in to the first exercise, let's set up the lab environment.

3.1 Setting up the Lab.

Software's and images used.

#	Item	Software
1	Lab simulation software	GNS3
2	Switches	Cisco L2 virtual
3	Network Automation PC	---

Since I used GNS3 as my lab platform, the switches are running the IOS virtual images. You can download the required cisco IOSv from the Cisco software downloads website. Also for running the Virtual IOS devices, you need to have the GNS Virtual machine installed on your machine as well.

The network automation PC is by default available inside GNS3. So when you install GNS3, the Network automation PC appliance will get automatically installed.

Important Links:

- Download GNS3: https://gns3.com/software
- To install Cisco IOSv on GNS3, refer to GNS3 documentation. https://docs.gns3.com/appliances/cisco-iosvl2.html
- Download the IOS images from Cisco Software downloads. https://software.cisco.com/download/

3.2 Topology

In this lab topology, I have used the following components in GNS3.

1) A Network Automation Appliance named as NetworkAutomation-PC.

We will be coding python in this PC.

2) A Layer2 Ethernet Switch named as AccessSW.

Used as a connection point for NetworkAutomation-PC, CoreSW and NAT cloud. There is no configuration for this switch as it's a generic L2 one.

3) A NAT cloud named as NAT-1. This is used to provide internet connectivity to the NetworkAutomation-PC. NAT-1 also acts as a DHCP server and it provides IP to NetworkAutomation-PC. Internet connectivity is not mandatory for this lab, however I update my NetworkAutomation-PC.

You can have the topology without the NAT cloud and in case you encounter any package or library missing errors while writing python code, then put the NAT cloud and update the Automation-PC to download the missing files.

4) Four Cisco Virtual IOS switches.

We will be configuring these 4 switches from our NetworkAutomation-PC using python programming.

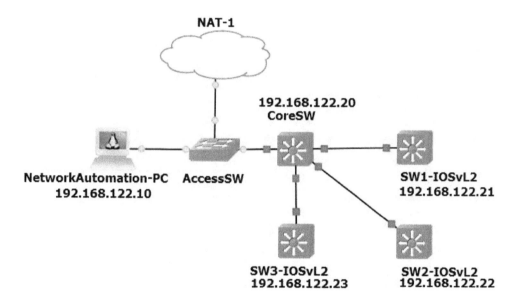

IP Details	
NetworkAutomation-PC	**192.168.122.10**
CoreSW	192.168.122.20
SW3	192.168.122.21
SW1	192.168.122.22
SW2	192.168.122.23

3.3 Configure the devices

Setting up the NetworkAutomation-PC.

You can configure the Automation-PC with either Static IP or DHCP IP.

In this lab, I have configured the NetworkAutomation-PC with a DHCP IP, which is received from NAT-1 Cloud.

1) Configure IP

The network configuration file is located at **/etc/network/ location**.
cat /etc/network/interfaces shows the current network interface information.
If you want to edit, then use a text editor such as **vi** or **nano.**
Edit the file,
nano /etc/network/interfaces

In order to configure the PC as a DHCP client, just uncomment he bottom two lines. That is,

```
# DHCP config for eth0
  auto eth0
  iface eth0 inet dhcp
```

Save the configuration and exit.
Now you need to restart the PC, I order to receive the DHCP IP address.
I have shown each steps in the following pictures.

NetworkAutomation-PC

```
GNU nano 2.5.3              File: /etc/network/interfaces

#
# This is a sample network config uncomment lines to configure the network
#


# Static config for eth0
#auto eth0
#iface eth0 inet static
#        address 192.168.10.2
#        netmask 255.255.255.0
#        gateway 192.168.10.1
#        up echo nameserver 192.168.10.1 > /etc/resolv.conf

# DHCP config for eth0
 auto eth0
 iface eth0 inet dhcp
```

Reload the Automation-PC, now you can see that the PC has been received with a DHCP IP., here it is 1921.68.122.10. You may receive a different IP based on your settings.

```
udhcpc (v1.24.2) started
Sending discover...
Sending discover...
Sending discover...
Sending select for 192.168.122.10...
Lease of 192.168.122.10 obtained, lease time 3600
root@NetworkAutomation-PC:~#
root@NetworkAutomation-PC:~#
root@NetworkAutomation-PC:~#
root@NetworkAutomation-PC:~#
```

Verify the Interface configuration using **ifconfig** command.

```
root@NetworkAutomation-PC:~# ifconfig
eth0      Link encap:Ethernet  HWaddr 06:ba:b1:09:5b:95
          inet addr:192.168.122.10  Bcast:192.168.122.255  Mask:255.255.255.0
          UP BROADCAST RUNNING MULTICAST  MTU:1500  Metric:1
          RX packets:18247 errors:0 dropped:10 overruns:0 frame:0
          TX packets:7590 errors:0 dropped:0 overruns:0 carrier:0
          collisions:0 txqueuelen:1000
          RX bytes:26573722 (26.5 MB)  TX bytes:416942 (416.9 KB)
```

Now the AutomationPC is configured with an IP address.
Next, configure each Cisco vIOS switches with an IP address.

As I mentioned in the pre-requisites section, knowledge of Cisco IOS commands are necessary for this lab. I hope you do have some experience with cisco devices.

2) Update the NetworkAutomation-PC (Optional but recommended)

Open the NetworkAutomation-PC console and issue **apt-get update** command.
Then it will communicated with internet and download the necessary updates.

```
root@NetworkAutomation-PC:~# apt-get update
Get:1 http://security.ubuntu.com/ubuntu xenial-security InRelease [107 kB]
Get:2 http://archive.ubuntu.com/ubuntu xenial InRelease [247 kB]
Get:3 http://ppa.launchpad.net/ansible/ansible-2.4/ubuntu xenial InRelease [18.0 kB]
Get:4 http://security.ubuntu.com/ubuntu xenial-security/universe Sources [93.8 kB]
Get:5 http://ppa.launchpad.net/ansible/ansible-2.4/ubuntu xenial/main amd64 Packages
Get:6 http://archive.ubuntu.com/ubuntu xenial-updates InRelease [109 kB]
Get:7 http://archive.ubuntu.com/ubuntu xenial-backports InRelease [107 kB]
Get:8 http://archive.ubuntu.com/ubuntu xenial/universe Sources [9802 kB]
Get:9 http://security.ubuntu.com/ubuntu xenial-security/main amd64 Packages [709 kB]
23% [8 Sources 2177 kB/9802 kB 22%] [9 Packages 495 kB/709 kB 70%]
```

3) Verify python version.

Note that, NetworkAutomation appliance is installed with both versions of python. That is version 2 and 3. IF you want to run codes using python3, then always prefix python3 <filename.py>

```
root@NetworkAutomation-PC:~# python
Python 2.7.12 (default, Dec  4 2017, 14:50:18)
[GCC 5.4.0 20160609] on linux2
Type "help", "copyright", "credits" or "license" for more information.
>>>
[3]+  Stopped                 python
root@NetworkAutomation-PC:~# python3
Python 3.5.2 (default, Nov 23 2017, 16:37:01)
[GCC 5.4.0 20160609] on linux
Type "help", "copyright", "credits" or "license" for more information.
>>>
```

2) Configure the switches.
Configure a management IP and then enable telnet on each switch.

First I'm configuring the CoreSW.
Open then console of CoreSW node.

```
Switch>en
Switch#conf t
Enter configuration commands, one per line.    End
with CNTL/Z.
←-Configure the enable password-→
Switch(config)#enable secret cisco
Switch(config)#
```

←-Configure the management IP address to VLAN1-→

```
Switch(config)#int vlan1
Switch(config-if)#ip          add          192.168.122.20
255.255.255.0
Switch(config-if)#no sh
Switch(config-if)#
Switch(config-if)#exit
```

←----------Configure Telnet--------------------------→

```
Switch(config)#line vty 0 4
Switch(config-line)#login local
Switch(config-line)#exit
Switch(config)#
Switch(config)#username cisco password cisco
Switch(config)#exit
Switch#
```

←----------------Save the Configuration----------------→

```
Switch#wr memory
Building configuration...
Compressed  configuration  from  3606  bytes  to  1622
bytes[OK]
Switch#
```

Try the reachability to the CoreSW from our NetworkAutomation-PC.

```
root@NetworkAutomation-PC:~# ping 192.168.122.20
PING 192.168.122.20 (192.168.122.20) 56(84) bytes of
data.
64  bytes  from  192.168.122.20:  icmp_seq=1  ttl=255
time=5.77 ms
64  bytes  from  192.168.122.20:  icmp_seq=2  ttl=255
time=4.55 ms.
```

So it reachable, and now try to telnet in to the switch.

```
root@NetworkAutomation-PC:~# telnet 192.168.122.20
Trying 192.168.122.20...
Connected to 192.168.122.20.
Escape character is '^]'.

********************************************************************
* IOSv is strictly limited to use for evaluation, demonstration and IOS  *
* education. IOSv is provided as-is and is not supported by Cisco's       *
* Technical Advisory Center. Any use or disclosure, in whole or in part,  *
* of the IOSv Software or Documentation to any third party for any        *
* purposes is expressly prohibited except as otherwise authorized by      *
* Cisco in writing.                                                       *
********************************************************************
User Access Verification

Username: cisco
Password:
********************************************************************
* IOSv is strictly limited to use for evaluation, demonstration and IOS  *
* education. IOSv is provided as-is and is not supported by Cisco's       *
* Technical Advisory Center. Any use or disclosure, in whole or in part,  *
* of the IOSv Software or Documentation to any third party for any        *
* purposes is expressly prohibited except as otherwise authorized by      *
* Cisco in writing.                                                       *
********************************************************************
Switch>en
Password:
Switch#
```

So the connectivity is ok.
Similarly Configure the remaining three switches (SW1,SW2 & SW3).

SW1 configuration

```
Switch>
Switch>en
Switch#conf t
Enter configuration commands, one per line.  End
with CNTL/Z.
Switch(config)#enable secret cisco
Switch(config)#int vlan1
Switch(config-if)#ip     address     192.168.122.21
255.255.255.0
Switch(config-if)#no sh
Switch(config-if)#
Switch(config)#username cisco password cisco
Switch(config)#line vty 0 4
Switch(config-line)#login local
Switch(config-line)#end
Switch#write memory
Building configuration...
```

SW2 configuration

```
Switch>
Switch>en
Switch#conf t
Enter configuration commands, one per line.  End
with CNTL/Z.
Switch(config)#enable secret cisco
Switch(config)#int vlan1
Switch(config-if)#ip      address     192.168.122.22
255.255.255.0
Switch(config-if)#no sh
Switch(config-if)#
Switch(config)#username cisco password cisco
Switch(config)#line vty 0 4
Switch(config-line)#login local
Switch(config-line)#end
Switch#write memory
Building configuration...
```

SW3 configuration

```
Switch>
Switch>en
Switch#conf t
Enter configuration commands, one per line.  End
with CNTL/Z.
Switch(config)#enable secret cisco
Switch(config)#int vlan1
Switch(config-if)#ip      address     192.168.122.23
255.255.255.0
Switch(config-if)#no sh
Switch(config-if)#
Switch(config)#username cisco password cisco
Switch(config)#line vty 0 4
Switch(config-line)#login local
Switch(config-line)#end
Switch#write memory
Building configuration...
```

Now I am able to telnet all the four switches from the NetworkAutomation-PC.

3.4 Writing the Python Code

While we write the python code, we may import and use many python packages and libraries made by various developers. Each of them have specific functionalities.

You will be seeing different libraries that I import in to the code. For example, for using telnet functions, we can import the libraries related to telnet. This not only saves time, but also make our code small and efficient.

You can search in the internet for more information on each library files.

We should have the basic understanding of the cisco IOS command and the expected output. Our code is aligned with these outputs.

For example: when we telnet in to a cisco switch, it will give a prompt "**Username :**". We write the code in such a way that, when the program encounter the exact match, it will perform something. Illustrated in the picture below.

Logically saying, if found "**Username :**" , then do this. If there is a typo error or a missing space, then the code won't work as you desired.

Exercise 1: Python code to Change the Hostname using telnet.

Below is the python code for achieving our task, that is changing the hostname. Write the code using a nano editor from NetworkAutomation-PC. **ex1.py** is the filename I used.

```
root@NetworkAutomation-PC:~#          nano          ex1.py
```

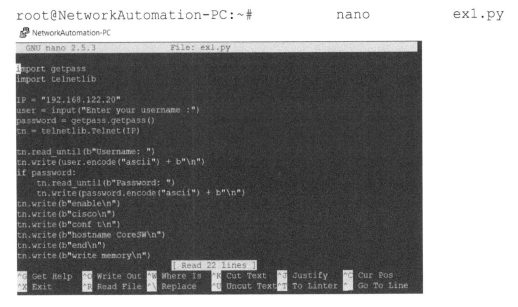

After executing the above command, you will be having an text editor and start writing the code.

First import the necessary library files using import command.

```
import getpass
```

```
import telnetlib
```

<--- Declare a variable for storing the IP address --->

```
IP = "localhost"
```

<--- Declare a variable for storing username --->

```
user = input("Enter your username :")
```

<---Use getpass module which we imported, to get the password from the user--->

```
password = getpass.getpass()
```

<--- Pass the IP variable value in to the telnetlib which we imported --->

```
tn = telnetlib.Telnet(IP)
```

<--- Python code works top to bottom. Now the code will read each output from the cisco switch and when it encounter the Username : statement, do the following --->

```
tn.read_until(b"Username: ")
```

<--- Remember, python3 bydefault uses unicode encoding. Here we have to use the ascii encoding because this has to be sent to the switch as ascii characters --->

```
tn.write(user.encode("ascii") + b"\n")

if password:

    tn.read_until(b"Password: ")

    tn.write(password.encode("ascii") + b"\n")
```

<--- Now specify the commands in the right sequence.enable password, then change to configuration terminal and change the hostname, finally ssave the configuration and exit--->

```
tn.write(b"enable\n")

tn.write(b"cisco\n")

tn.write(b"conf t\n")

tn.write(b"hostname CoreSW\n")

tn.write(b"end\n")

tn.write(b"write memory\n")

tn.write(b"exit\n")
```

<--- read_all() function will show the output on your screen after decoding the ascii to unicode.--->

```
print(tn.read_all().decode('ascii'))
```

Save the code and exit.
Now run the code from Automation-PC. You can see the output as follows.

```
root@NetworkAutomation-PC:~# python3 ex1.py
Enter your username :cisco
Password:

**************************************************************
* IOSv is strictly limited to use for evaluation, demonstration and IOS   *
* education. IOSv is provided as-is and is not supported by Cisco's        *
* Technical Advisory Center. Any use or disclosure, in whole or in part,   *
* of the IOSv Software or Documentation to any third party for any         *
* purposes is expressly prohibited except as otherwise authorized by       *
* Cisco in writing.                                                        *
**************************************************************
Switch>enable
Password:
Switch#conf t
Enter configuration commands, one per line.  End with CNTL/Z.
Switch(config)#hostname CoreSW
CoreSW(config)#end
CoreSW#write memory
Building configuration...
Compressed configuration from 3662 bytes to 1682 bytes[OK]
CoreSW#exit

root@NetworkAutomation-PC:~#
```

Verify the change on the switch. You can see that the hostname has been successfully changed.

```
*Sep 26 17:47:00.872: %SYS-5-CONFIG_I: Configured from console by cisco on vty0 (192.168.122.10)
*Sep 26 17:47:04.147: %GRUB-5-CONFIG_WRITING: GRUB configuration is being updated on disk. Please wait...
*Sep 26 17:47:04.876: %GRUB-5-CONFIG_WRITTEN: GRUB configuration was written to disk successfully.
*********************************************************
* IOSv is strictly limited to use for evaluation, demonstration and IOS   *
* education. IOSv is provided as-is and is not supported by Cisco's        *
* Technical Advisory Center. Any use or disclosure, in whole or in part,   *
* of the IOSv Software or Documentation to any third party for any         *
* purposes is expressly prohibited except as otherwise authorized by       *
* Cisco in writing.                                                        *
*********************************************************
CoreSW>
CoreSW>
CoreSW>
```

Exercise1 : Summary.

Python Code

```python
import getpass
import telnetlib

IP = "localhost"
user = input("Enter your username :")
password = getpass.getpass()
tn = telnetlib.Telnet(IP)

tn.read_until(b"Username: ")
tn.write(user.encode("ascii") + b"\n")
if password:
    tn.read_until(b"Password: ")
```

```
    tn.write(password.encode("ascii") + b"\n")
tn.write(b"enable\n")
tn.write(b"cisco\n")
tn.write(b"conf t\n")
tn.write(b"hostname CoreSW\n")
tn.write(b"end\n")
tn.write(b"write memory\n")
tn.write(b"exit\n")

print(tn.read_all().decode('ascii'))
```

Execute the Code

```
root@NetworkAutomation-PC:~# python3 ex1.py
Enter your username :cisco
Password:


**********************************************************
****************
*  IOSv  is  strictly  limited  to  use  for  evaluation,
demonstration and IOS  *
* education. IOSv is provided as-is and is not supported
by Cisco's       *
* Technical Advisory Center. Any use or disclosure, in
whole or in part, *
* of the IOSv Software or Documentation to any third
party for any        *
* purposes is expressly prohibited except as otherwise
authorized by      *
*              Cisco              in              writing.
*
**********************************************************
****************
Switch>enable
Password:
Switch#conf t
Enter configuration commands, one per line.  End with
CNTL/Z.
Switch(config)#hostname CoreSW
CoreSW(config)#end
CoreSW#write memory
Building configuration...
Compressed  configuration  from  3662  bytes  to  1682
bytes[OK]
CoreSW#exit
```

```
root@NetworkAutomation-PC:~#
```

Similarly do the same for all the switches.

Exercise 2: Python code to get the running configuration.

Write the following code in the text editor from NetworkAutomation-PC.

```python
import getpass
import telnetlib

IP = input("Enter the IP Address :")
user = input("Enter your username :")
password = getpass.getpass()
tn = telnetlib.Telnet(IP)

tn.read_until(b"Username: ")
tn.write(user.encode("ascii") + b"\n")
if password:
    tn.read_until(b"Password: ")
    tn.write(password.encode("ascii") + b"\n")
tn.write(b"enable\n")
tn.write(b"cisco\n")
tn.write(b"show run\n")
tn.write(b"end\n")
tn.write(b"exit\n")

print(tn.read_all().decode('ascii'))
```

Execute the code and you will be prompted to enter the IP address.

```
root@NetworkAutomation-PC:~# nano ex2.py
root@NetworkAutomation-PC:~# python3 ex2.py
Enter the IP Address :192.168.122.20
Enter your username :cisco
Password:
```

Compare the following code with the Exercise1 code. What are the differences that you observed?

Exercise2: Summary.

Code summary

```
import getpass
import telnetlib

IP = input("Enter the IP Address :")
user = input("Enter your username :")
password = getpass.getpass()
tn = telnetlib.Telnet(IP)

tn.read_until(b"Username: ")
tn.write(user.encode("ascii") + b"\n")
if password:
    tn.read_until(b"Password: ")
    tn.write(password.encode("ascii") + b"\n")
tn.write(b"enable\n")
tn.write(b"cisco\n")
tn.write(b"show run\n")
tn.write(b"\n")
tn.write(b"exit\n")

print(tn.read_all().decode('ascii'))
```

Execute the code: Output:

```
root@NetworkAutomation-PC:~# nano ex2.py
root@NetworkAutomation-PC:~# python3 ex2.py
Enter the IP Address :192.168.122.20
Enter your username :cisco
Password:

**********************************************************
*****************
*  IOSv  is  strictly  limited  to  use  for  evaluation,
demonstration and IOS  *
* education. IOSv is provided as-is and is not supported
by Cisco's       *
* Technical Advisory Center. Any use or disclosure, in
whole or in part, *
* of  the  IOSv  Software  or  Documentation  to  any  third
party for any       *
* purposes  is  expressly  prohibited  except  as  otherwise
authorized by       *
*              Cisco              in              writing.
*
```

```
* * * * * * * * * * * * * * * * * * * * * * * * * * * * * * * * * * * * * * * * * * * * * * * * * * *
* * * * * * * * * * * * * * * *
CoreSW>enable
Password:
CoreSW#show run
Building configuration...

Current configuration : 3662 bytes
!
! Last configuration change at 17:47:00 UTC Wed Sep 26
2018 by cisco
!
version 15.2
service timestamps debug datetime msec
service timestamps log datetime msec
no service password-encryption
service compress-config
!
hostname CoreSW
!
boot-start-marker
boot-end-marker
!
!
enable secret 5 $1$OtfS$bV3p/pOdjKkOFlahCt0GA1
!
username cisco password 0 cisco
no aaa new-model
!
!

CoreSW#exit

root@NetworkAutomation-PC:~#
```

Exercise 3: Create and assign IP to a VLAN interface.

```
import getpass
import telnetlib

IP = input("Enter the IP Address :")
user = input("Enter your username :")
password = getpass.getpass()
```

```
tn = telnetlib.Telnet(IP)

tn.read_until(b"Username: ")
tn.write(user.encode("ascii") + b"\n")
if password:
    tn.read_until(b"Password: ")
    tn.write(password.encode("ascii") + b"\n")
tn.write(b"enable\n")
tn.write(b"cisco\n")
tn.write(b"conf t\n")
tn.write(b"vlan 20\n")
tn.write(b"name Data_VLAN_20\n")
tn.write(b"int vlan 20\n")
tn.write(b"ip add 10.20.30.40 255.255.255.0\n")
tn.write(b"no sh\n")
tn.write(b"end\n")
tn.write(b"show ip int br\n")
tn.write(b"exit\n")

print(tn.read_all().decode('ascii'))
```

Execute the code: Output:
```
root@NetworkAutomation-PC:~# nano ex3.py
root@NetworkAutomation-PC:~# python3 ex3.py
Enter the IP Address :192.168.122.20
Enter your username :cisco
Password:

*************************************************************
*****************
*  IOSv  is  strictly  limited  to  use  for  evaluation,
demonstration and IOS  *
* education. IOSv is provided as-is and is not supported
by Cisco's        *
* Technical Advisory Center. Any use or disclosure, in
whole or in part, *
*  of  the  IOSv  Software  or  Documentation  to  any  third
party for any        *
* purposes is expressly prohibited except as otherwise
authorized by      *
*              Cisco              in              writing.
*
*************************************************************
*****************
```

```
CoreSW>enable
Password:
CoreSW#conf t
Enter configuration commands, one per line.  End with
CNTL/Z.
CoreSW(config)#vlan 20
CoreSW(config-vlan)#name Data_VLAN_20
CoreSW(config-vlan)#int vlan 20
CoreSW(config-if)#ip add 10.20.30.40 255.255.255.0
CoreSW(config-if)#no sh
CoreSW(config-if)#end
CoreSW#show ip int br
```

Interface	IP-Address	OK?	Method	Status	Protocol
GigabitEthernet0/0	unassigned	YES	unset	up	up
GigabitEthernet0/1	unassigned	YES	unset	up	up
GigabitEthernet0/2	unassigned	YES	unset	up	up
GigabitEthernet0/3	unassigned	YES	unset	up	up
GigabitEthernet1/0	unassigned	YES	unset	up	up
GigabitEthernet1/1	unassigned	YES	unset	up	up
GigabitEthernet1/2	unassigned	YES	unset	up	up
GigabitEthernet1/3	unassigned	YES	unset	up	up
GigabitEthernet2/0	unassigned	YES	unset	up	up
GigabitEthernet2/1	unassigned	YES	unset	up	up
GigabitEthernet2/2	unassigned	YES	unset	up	up
GigabitEthernet2/3	unassigned	YES	unset	up	up
GigabitEthernet3/0	unassigned	YES	unset	up	up
GigabitEthernet3/1	unassigned	YES	unset	up	up
GigabitEthernet3/2	unassigned	YES	unset	up	up

```
GigabitEthernet3/3          unassigned          YES unset   up
up
Vlan1                       192.168.122.20  YES manual  up
up
Vlan20                      10.20.30.40     YES manual  down
down
CoreSW#exit

root@NetworkAutomation-PC:~#
```

```
coresw(config-vlan)#name data_vlan
coresw(config-vlan)#exit
coresw(config)#
*Sep 26 19:04:58.044: %SYS-5-CONFIG_I: Configured from console by cisco on vty0 (192.168.122.10)
*Sep 26 19:04:58.678: %LINEPROTO-5-UPDOWN: Line protocol on Interface Vlan20, changed state to down
*Sep 26 19:04:59.928: %LINK-3-UPDOWN: Interface Vlan20, changed state to down
*Sep 26 19:07:06.234: %SYS-5-CONFIG_I: Configured from console by cisco on vty1 (192.168.122.10)
```

You can see the VLAN 20 has been created by running the python code. The catch here is, you should know the commands well and should know the sequence as well.

Additional tasks

Now you should be knowing how to automate the cisco commands using python code. Try the following tasks, and please do it so that you will be good with the concepts. I am not providing the codes for this. If you are able to understand the first 3 exercises, then these tasks should be easy for you.

1) Create a loopback interface and assign an IP, then get the running config.
2) Create a new user.
3) Delete the previously created VLAN 20.

Exercise 4: Create multiple VLANs using python for loop.

At this point, I assume that you already have a basic idea about for loops. If you don't, please feel free to go to the Loops section under "**Understand the Basics**" section.

In this exercise, we need to create an additional eight VLANS ranging from 2 to 9. We can create a script for creating multiple VLANs one by one manually. But that is tedious and not a good idea while writing a python code.

For achieving our goal, we are going to use a **for loop** in our code.

In the below picture, you can see that the switch only has the default VLANs and VLAN 20.

```
CoreSW#show vlan br

VLAN Name                             Status    Ports
---- -------------------------------- --------- -------------------------------
1    default                          active    Gi0/0, Gi0/1, Gi0/2, Gi0/3
                                                Gi1/0, Gi1/1, Gi1/2, Gi1/3
                                                Gi2/0, Gi2/1, Gi2/2, Gi2/3
                                                Gi3/0, Gi3/1, Gi3/2, Gi3/3
20   Data_VLAN_20                     active
1002 fddi-default                     act/unsup
1003 token-ring-default               act/unsup
1004 fddinet-default                  act/unsup
1005 trnet-default                    act/unsup
CoreSW#
CoreSW#
```

```python
import getpass
import telnetlib


IP = input("Enter the IP Address :")
user = input("Enter your username :")
password = getpass.getpass()
tn = telnetlib.Telnet(IP)


tn.read_until(b"Username: ")
tn.write(user.encode("ascii") + b"\n")
if password:
    tn.read_until(b"Password: ")
    tn.write(password.encode("ascii") + b"\n")
tn.write(b"enable\n")
tn.write(b"cisco\n")
tn.write(b"conf t\n")
```

<--- Create a for loop to create multiple VLANs in a go. In python2, the default encoding is ASCII but in Python3, the default encoding is Unicode. This is the reason, why we need to put the encoding command,to convert in to ASCII characters. Also note that we are converting the value on n to string value using str() command. --->

<--- Be careful about indentations. Python does care those white spaces and if you put it improperly, then your code wont work. --->

```python
for n in range (2, 10):
    tn.write(b"vlan  " + str(n).encode("ascii") + b"\n")
```

```
        tn.write(b"name         Data_VLAN_"              +
str(n).encode("ascii") + b"\n")
```

```
tn.write(b"conf t\n")
for n in range (2, 10):
    tn.write(b"vlan " + str(n).encode("ascii") + b"\n")
    tn.write(b"name Data_VLAN_" + str(n).encode("ascii") + b"\n")
tn.write(b"end\n")
tn.write(b"show vlan br\n\n")
tn.write(b"exit\n")

print(tn.read_all().decode('ascii'))
```

<--- So the for loop is checking a range from 2 to 10. This checking will begin with number 2 and keep increment until 10. But 10 is not included. --->

```
tn.write(b"end\n")
tn.write(b"show vlan br\n\n")
tn.write(b"exit\n")

print(tn.read_all().decode("ascii"))
```

Now run the code. It might take some time to complete the entire operation.

Once it run successfully, you can see that the new VLANs are created on the Switch as we intended.

```
CoreSW#show vlan br

VLAN Name                             Status    Ports
---- -------------------------------- --------- -------------------------------
1    default                          active    Gi0/0, Gi0/1, Gi0/2, Gi0/3
                                                Gi1/0, Gi1/1, Gi1/2, Gi1/3
                                                Gi2/0, Gi2/1, Gi2/2, Gi2/3
                                                Gi3/0, Gi3/1, Gi3/2, Gi3/3
2    Data_VLAN_2                      active
3    Data_VLAN_3                      active
4    Data_VLAN_4                      active
5    Data_VLAN_5                      active
6    Data_VLAN_6                      active
7    Data_VLAN_7                      active
8    Data_VLAN_8                      active
9    Data_VLAN_9                      active
20   Data_VLAN_20                     active
1002 fddi-default                     act/unsup
1003 token-ring-default               act/unsup
1004 fddinet-default                  act/unsup
1005 trnet-default                    act/unsup
CoreSW#
```

Exercise 4: Summary

Code Summary

```
import getpass
import telnetlib
```

```
IP = input("Enter the IP Address :")
user = input("Enter your username :")
password = getpass.getpass()
tn = telnetlib.Telnet(IP)
tn.read_until(b"Username: ")
tn.write(user.encode("ascii") + b"\n")
if password:
    tn.read_until(b"Password: ")
    tn.write(password.encode("ascii") + b"\n")
tn.write(b"enable\n")
tn.write(b"cisco\n")
tn.write(b"conf t\n")
for n in range (2, 10):
    tn.write(b"vlan   "  +   str(n).encode("ascii")   +
b"\n")
    tn.write(b"name            Data_VLAN_"            +
str(n).encode("ascii") + b"\n")
tn.write(b"end\n")
tn.write(b"show vlan br\n\n")
tn.write(b"exit\n")

print(tn.read_all().decode('ascii'))
```

Execute the code: Output:

```
root@NetworkAutomation-PC:~# nano ex4.py
root@NetworkAutomation-PC:~# python3 ex4.py
Enter the IP Address :192.168.122.20
Enter your username :cisco
Password:

**************************************************
********************
* IOSv is strictly limited to use for evaluation,
demonstration and IOS  *
* education. IOSv is provided as-is and is not
supported by Cisco's      *
* Technical Advisory Center. Any use or disclosure,
in whole or in part,  *
```

```
* of the IOSv Software or Documentation to any third
party for any          *
*  purposes  is  expressly  prohibited  except  as
otherwise authorized by      *
*              Cisco              in              writing.
*
*******************************************************
*********************
CoreSW>enable
Password:
CoreSW#conf t
Enter configuration commands, one per line.  End
with CNTL/Z.
CoreSW(config)#vlan 2
CoreSW(config-vlan)#name Data_VLAN_2
CoreSW(config-vlan)#vlan 3
CoreSW(config-vlan)#name Data_VLAN_3
CoreSW(config-vlan)#vlan 4
CoreSW(config-vlan)#name Data_VLAN_4
CoreSW(config-vlan)#vlan 5
CoreSW(config-vlan)#name Data_VLAN_5
CoreSW(config-vlan)#vlan 6
CoreSW(config-vlan)#name Data_VLAN_6
CoreSW(config-vlan)#vlan 7
CoreSW(config-vlan)#name Data_VLAN_7
CoreSW(config-vlan)#vlan 8
CoreSW(config-vlan)#name Data_VLAN_8
CoreSW(config-vlan)#vlan 9
CoreSW(config-vlan)#name Data_VLAN_9
CoreSW(config-vlan)#end
CoreSW#show vlan br

VLAN Name                                        Status
Ports
---- -------------------------------- --------- ----
---------------------------
1    default                                     active
Gi0/0, Gi0/1, Gi0/2, Gi0/3

Gi1/0, Gi1/1, Gi1/2, Gi1/3
```

```
Gi2/0, Gi2/1, Gi2/2, Gi2/3

Gi3/0, Gi3/1, Gi3/2, Gi3/3
2    Data_VLAN_2                          active
3    Data_VLAN_3                          active
4    Data_VLAN_4                          active
5    Data_VLAN_5                          active
6    Data_VLAN_6                          active
7    Data_VLAN_7                          active
8    Data_VLAN_8                          active
9    Data_VLAN_9                          active
20   Data_VLAN_20                         active
1002 fddi-default                         act/unsup
1003 token-ring-default                   act/unsup
1004 fddinet-default                      act/unsup
1005 trnet-default                        act/unsup
CoreSW#
CoreSW#exit

root@NetworkAutomation-PC:~#
```

Exercise 5: Create multiple VLANs on multiple switches.

In this exercise, we are going to do configuration changes to all four switches in our lab using a single script.

For this, first we need to create afile containing the IP addresses of all the four switches. Later in the program, we will call this file and the code will check IP one by one and perform the operation.

Create a file named as switches.txt. Write all the four IP address of the switches in the test file, one by one. Then save and exit.

```
root@NetworkAutomation-PC:~# nano switches.txt
```

NetworkAutomation-PC

```
 GNU nano 2.5.3                      File: switches.txt

192.168.122.20
192.168.122.21
192.168.122.22
192.168.122.23
```

Verify that your file is created and available at the location.

```
root@NetworkAutomation-PC:~# ls -l
total 28
-rw-r--r-- 1 root root 511 Sep 26 17:49 ex1.py
-rw-r--r-- 1 root root 511 Sep 26 18:15 ex1_a.py
-rw-r--r-- 1 root root 468 Sep 26 18:27 ex2.py
-rw-r--r-- 1 root root 650 Sep 26 19:12 ex3.py
-rw-r--r-- 1 root root 642 Sep 26 22:20 ex4.py
-rw-r--r-- 1 root root 667 Sep 26 23:40 ex5.py
-rw-r--r-- 1 root root  60 Sep 26 23:34 switches.txt
root@NetworkAutomation-PC:~#
```

Lets understand the code,

```
import getpass
import telnetlib
```

<--- Since my credentials for all four switches are same, i let the user prompt to enter the password at the beginning of the code. If the credentials are different for each switches, put the code inside the for loop --->

```
user = input("Enter your username :")
password = getpass.getpass()
```

<--- Load and open the switches.txt file in the code. --->

```
f = open("switches.txt")
```

<--- For loop will get the IP from the switches.txt file one by one and execute the code block. Once again , please note the indentations. . --->

```
for IP in f:
    IP = IP.strip()
    print("Configuring Switch " + (IP))
```

```
tn = telnetlib.Telnet(IP)
tn.read_until(b"Username: ")
tn.write(user.encode("ascii") + b"\n")
if password:
    tn.read_until(b"Password: ")
    tn.write(password.encode("ascii") + b"\n")
tn.write(b"enable\n")
tn.write(b"cisco\n")
tn.write(b"conf t\n")
for n in range (2, 10):
    tn.write(b"vlan " + str(n).encode("ascii") + b"\n")
    tn.write(b"name Data_VLAN_" + str(n).encode("ascii") +
    b"\n")
tn.write(b"end\n")
tn.write(b"show vlan br\n\n")
tn.write(b"exit\n")
print(tn.read_all().decode("ascii"))
```

```
user = input("Enter your username :")
password = getpass.getpass()

f = open("switches.txt")
for IP in f:
    IP = IP.strip()
    print("Configuring Switch " + (IP))
    tn = telnetlib.Telnet(IP)
    tn.read_until(b"Username: ")
    tn.write(user.encode("ascii") + b"\n")
    if password:
        tn.read_until(b"Password: ")
        tn.write(password.encode("ascii") + b"\n")
    tn.write(b"enable\n")
    tn.write(b"cisco\n")
    tn.write(b"conf t\n")
```

Once you run the code, it will configure all the four switches in a matter of seconds.

Exercise 5: Summary

Code Summary

```
import getpass
```

```
import telnetlib

user = input("Enter your username :")
password = getpass.getpass()

f = open("switches.txt")
for IP in f:
    IP = IP.strip()
    print("Configuring Switch " + (IP))
    tn = telnetlib.Telnet(IP)
    tn.read_until(b"Username: ")
    tn.write(user.encode("ascii") + b"\n")
    if password:
        tn.read_until(b"Password: ")
        tn.write(password.encode("ascii") + b"\n")
    tn.write(b"enable\n")
    tn.write(b"cisco\n")
    tn.write(b"conf t\n")
    for n in range (2, 10):
        tn.write(b"vlan " + str(n).encode("ascii") +
        b"\n")  #continuation of the above line
        tn.write(b"name Data_VLAN_" +
        str(n).encode("ascii") +   b"\n")  #continuation of the
above line
    tn.write(b"end\n")
    tn.write(b"show vlan br\n\n")
    tn.write(b"exit\n")
    print(tn.read_all().decode("ascii"))
```

Execute Code: Output

```
root@NetworkAutomation-PC:~# python3 ex5.py
Enter your username :cisco
Password:
Configuring Switch 192.168.122.20

**************************************************
*******************
* IOSv is strictly limited to use for evaluation,
demonstration and IOS   *
```

```
*  education.  IOSv  is  provided  as-is  and  is  not
supported by Cisco's        *
* Technical Advisory Center. Any use  or  disclosure,
in whole or in part, *
* of the IOSv Software or Documentation to any third
party for any        *
*  purposes  is  expressly  prohibited  except  as
otherwise authorized by      *
*             Cisco            in            writing.
*
* * * * * * * * * * * * * * * * * * * * * * * * * * * * * * * * * * * * * * * * * * * * * * * * * * *
* * * * * * * * * * * * * * * * * * * * *
CoreSW>enable
Password:
CoreSW#conf t
Enter  configuration  commands,  one  per  line.    End
with CNTL/Z.
CoreSW(config)#vlan 2
CoreSW(config-vlan)#name Data_VLAN_2
CoreSW(config-vlan)#vlan 3
CoreSW(config-vlan)#name Data_VLAN_3
CoreSW(config-vlan)#vlan 4
CoreSW(config-vlan)#name Data_VLAN_4
CoreSW(config-vlan)#vlan 5
CoreSW(config-vlan)#name Data_VLAN_5
CoreSW(config-vlan)#vlan 6
CoreSW(config-vlan)#name Data_VLAN_6
CoreSW(config-vlan)#vlan 7
CoreSW(config-vlan)#name Data_VLAN_7
CoreSW(config-vlan)#vlan 8
CoreSW(config-vlan)#name Data_VLAN_8
CoreSW(config-vlan)#vlan 9
CoreSW(config-vlan)#name Data_VLAN_9
CoreSW(config-vlan)#end
CoreSW#show vlan br

VLAN Name                                       Status
Ports
---- -------------------------------- --------- ----
-------------------------
```

```
1     default                              active
Gi0/0, Gi0/1, Gi0/2, Gi0/3

Gi1/0, Gi1/1, Gi1/2, Gi1/3

Gi2/0, Gi2/1, Gi2/2, Gi2/3

Gi3/0, Gi3/1, Gi3/2, Gi3/3
2     Data_VLAN_2                          active
3     Data_VLAN_3                          active
4     Data_VLAN_4                          active
5     Data_VLAN_5                          active
6     Data_VLAN_6                          active
7     Data_VLAN_7                          active
8     Data_VLAN_8                          active
9     Data_VLAN_9                          active
20    Data_VLAN_20                         active
1002  fddi-default                         act/unsup
1003  token-ring-default                   act/unsup
1004  fddinet-default                      act/unsup
1005  trnet-default                        act/unsup
CoreSW#
CoreSW#exit

Configuring Switch 192.168.122.21

**********************************************************
********************
* IOSv is strictly limited to use for evaluation,
demonstration and IOS  *
* education. IOSv is provided as-is and is  not
supported by Cisco's        *
* Technical Advisory Center. Any use or disclosure,
in whole or in part, *
* of the IOSv Software or Documentation to any third
party for any        *
* purposes is expressly prohibited  except  as
otherwise authorized by       *
*            Cisco             in             writing.
*
```

```
* * * * * * * * * * * * * * * * * * * * * * * * * * * * * * * * * * * * * * * * * * * * * * * * * *
* * * * * * * * * * * * * * * * * * * * * *
Switch>enable
Password:
Switch#conf t
Enter configuration commands, one per line.   End
with CNTL/Z.
Switch(config)#vlan 2
Switch(config-vlan)#name Data_VLAN_2
Switch(config-vlan)#vlan 3
Switch(config-vlan)#name Data_VLAN_3
Switch(config-vlan)#vlan 4
Switch(config-vlan)#name Data_VLAN_4
Switch(config-vlan)#vlan 5
Switch(config-vlan)#name Data_VLAN_5
Switch(config-vlan)#vlan 6
Switch(config-vlan)#name Data_VLAN_6
Switch(config-vlan)#vlan 7
Switch(config-vlan)#name Data_VLAN_7
Switch(config-vlan)#vlan 8
Switch(config-vlan)#name Data_VLAN_8
Switch(config-vlan)#vlan 9
Switch(config-vlan)#name Data_VLAN_9
Switch(config-vlan)#end
Switch#show vlan br

VLAN Name                                          Status
Ports
---- -------------------------------- --------- ----
--------------------------
1    default                                       active
Gi0/0, Gi0/1, Gi0/2, Gi0/3

Gi1/0, Gi1/1, Gi1/2, Gi1/3

Gi2/0, Gi2/1, Gi2/2, Gi2/3

Gi3/0, Gi3/1, Gi3/2, Gi3/3
2    Data_VLAN_2                          active
3    Data_VLAN_3                          active
4    Data_VLAN_4                          active
```

```
5     Data_VLAN_5                          active
6     Data_VLAN_6                          active
7     Data_VLAN_7                          active
8     Data_VLAN_8                          active
9     Data_VLAN_9                          active
1002 fddi-default                          act/unsup
1003 token-ring-default                    act/unsup
1004 fddinet-default                       act/unsup
1005 trnet-default                         act/unsup
Switch#
Switch#exit

Configuring Switch 192.168.122.22

*****************************************************
**********************
*  IOSv is strictly limited to use for evaluation,
demonstration and IOS   *
*  education. IOSv is provided as-is and is not
supported by Cisco's        *
* Technical Advisory Center. Any use or disclosure,
in whole or in part, *
* of the IOSv Software or Documentation to any third
party for any          *
*   purposes is expressly prohibited except  as
otherwise authorized by      *
*              Cisco              in             writing.
*
*****************************************************
**********************
Switch>enable
Password:
Switch#conf t
Enter configuration commands, one per line.   End
with CNTL/Z.
Switch(config)#vlan 2
Switch(config-vlan)#name Data_VLAN_2
Switch(config-vlan)#vlan 3
Switch(config-vlan)#name Data_VLAN_3
Switch(config-vlan)#vlan 4
Switch(config-vlan)#name Data_VLAN_4
```

```
Switch(config-vlan)#vlan 5
Switch(config-vlan)#name Data_VLAN_5
Switch(config-vlan)#vlan 6
Switch(config-vlan)#name Data_VLAN_6
Switch(config-vlan)#vlan 7
Switch(config-vlan)#name Data_VLAN_7
Switch(config-vlan)#vlan 8
Switch(config-vlan)#name Data_VLAN_8
Switch(config-vlan)#vlan 9
Switch(config-vlan)#name Data_VLAN_9
Switch(config-vlan)#end
Switch#show vlan br

VLAN Name                                 Status
Ports
---- -------------------------------- --------- ----
--------------------------
1    default                              active
Gi0/0, Gi0/1, Gi0/2, Gi0/3

Gi1/0, Gi1/1, Gi1/2, Gi1/3

Gi2/0, Gi2/1, Gi2/2, Gi2/3

Gi3/0, Gi3/1, Gi3/2, Gi3/3
2    Data_VLAN_2                    active
3    Data_VLAN_3                    active
4    Data_VLAN_4                    active
5    Data_VLAN_5                    active
6    Data_VLAN_6                    active
7    Data_VLAN_7                    active
8    Data_VLAN_8                    active
9    Data_VLAN_9                    active
1002 fddi-default                      act/unsup
1003 token-ring-default                act/unsup
1004 fddinet-default                   act/unsup
1005 trnet-default                     act/unsup
Switch#
Switch#exit

Configuring Switch 192.168.122.23
```

```
**********************************************
*********************
*  IOSv  is  strictly  limited  to  use  for  evaluation,
demonstration and IOS   *
*  education.  IOSv  is  provided  as-is  and  is  not
supported by Cisco's      *
* Technical Advisory Center. Any use  or  disclosure,
in whole or in part, *
* of the IOSv Software or Documentation to any third
party for any        *
*  purposes  is  expressly  prohibited  except  as
otherwise authorized by      *
*            Cisco            in           writing.
*
**********************************************
*********************
Switch>enable
Password:
Switch#conf t
Enter  configuration  commands,  one  per  line.   End
with CNTL/Z.
Switch(config)#vlan 2
Switch(config-vlan)#name Data_VLAN_2
Switch(config-vlan)#vlan 3
Switch(config-vlan)#name Data_VLAN_3
Switch(config-vlan)#vlan 4
Switch(config-vlan)#name Data_VLAN_4
Switch(config-vlan)#vlan 5
Switch(config-vlan)#name Data_VLAN_5
Switch(config-vlan)#vlan 6
Switch(config-vlan)#name Data_VLAN_6
Switch(config-vlan)#vlan 7
Switch(config-vlan)#name Data_VLAN_7
Switch(config-vlan)#vlan 8
Switch(config-vlan)#name Data_VLAN_8
Switch(config-vlan)#vlan 9
Switch(config-vlan)#name Data_VLAN_9
Switch(config-vlan)#end
Switch#show vlan br
```

```
VLAN Name                                  Status
Ports
---- -------------------------------- --------- ----
--------------------------
1     default                              active
Gi0/0, Gi0/1, Gi0/2, Gi0/3

Gi1/0, Gi1/1, Gi1/2, Gi1/3

Gi2/0, Gi2/1, Gi2/2, Gi2/3

Gi3/0, Gi3/1, Gi3/2, Gi3/3
2     Data_VLAN_2                    active
3     Data_VLAN_3                    active
4     Data_VLAN_4                    active
5     Data_VLAN_5                    active
6     Data_VLAN_6                    active
7     Data_VLAN_7                    active
8     Data_VLAN_8                    active
9     Data_VLAN_9                    active
1002 fddi-default                    act/unsup
1003 token-ring-default              act/unsup
1004 fddinet-default                 act/unsup
1005 trnet-default                   act/unsup
Switch#
Switch#exit

root@NetworkAutomation-PC:~#
```

Exercise 6: Configure SSH on all switches using python code.

Now configure SSH on all the switches. The concept is the same with the last exercise. This should be easy for you if you understand and practiced the previous exercises well.

So for configuring SSH on a switch, we need to create the key pairs,. Remember if there is a confirmation prompt with a particular command, for example; If the switch prompt a confirmation **"do you want to continue? Y/N",** you should keep this in your mind and write code accordingly as well. On such instances, If you don't include an enter/return or Y/N in your code, the python code will stuck that that point.

Code:

```
import getpass
import telnetlib

user = input("Enter your username :")
password = getpass.getpass()

f = open("switches.txt")
for IP in f:
    IP = IP.strip()
    print("Configuring Switch " + (IP))
    tn = telnetlib.Telnet(IP)
    tn.read_until(b"Username: ")
    tn.write(user.encode("ascii") + b"\n")
    if password:
        tn.read_until(b"Password: ")
        tn.write(password.encode("ascii") + b"\n")
    tn.write(b"enable\n")
    tn.write(b"cisco\n")
    tn.write(b"conf t\n")
    tn.write(b"ip domain-name jaacostan.com\n")
    tn.write(b"crypto key generate rsa modulus 1024\n\n")
    tn.write(b"line vty 0 4\n")
    tn.write(b"transport input ssh telnet\n")
    tn.write(b"end\n")
    tn.write(b"write memory\n")
    tn.write(b"exit\n")
    print(tn.read_all().decode("ascii"))
```

Execute the code: Output

```
root@NetworkAutomation-PC:~# nano ex6.py
root@NetworkAutomation-PC:~# python3 ex6.py
Enter your username :cisco
Password:
Configuring Switch 192.168.122.20

*************************************************************
****************
*  IOSv  is  strictly  limited  to  use  for  evaluation,
demonstration and IOS  *
* education. IOSv is provided as-is and is not supported
by Cisco's       *
```

```
* Technical Advisory Center. Any use or disclosure, in
whole or in part, *
* of the IOSv Software or Documentation to any third
party for any        *
* purposes is expressly prohibited except as otherwise
authorized by      *
*              Cisco              in              writing.
*
* * * * * * * * * * * * * * * * * * * * * * * * * * * * * * * * * * * * * * * * * * * * * * * * * * * * * * * * * * *
* * * * * * * * * * * * * * * *
CoreSW>enable
Password:
CoreSW#conf t
Enter configuration commands, one per line.  End with
CNTL/Z.
CoreSW(config)#ip domain-name jaacostan.com
CoreSW(config)#crypto key generate rsa modulus 1024
The name for the keys will be: CoreSW.jaacostan.com

% The key modulus size is 1024 bits
% Generating 1024 bit RSA keys, keys will be non-
exportable...
[OK] (elapsed time was 1 seconds)

CoreSW(config)#
CoreSW(config)#line vty 0 4
CoreSW(config-line)#transport input ssh telnet
CoreSW(config-line)#end
CoreSW#write memory
Building configuration...
Compressed   configuration   from   3776   bytes   to   1761
bytes[OK]
CoreSW#exit

Configuring Switch 192.168.122.21

* * * * * * * * * * * * * * * * * * * * * * * * * * * * * * * * * * * * * * * * * * * * * * * * * * * * * * * * *
* * * * * * * * * * * * * * * *
* IOSv is strictly limited to use for evaluation,
demonstration and IOS  *
* education. IOSv is provided as-is and is not supported
by Cisco's      *
* Technical Advisory Center. Any use or disclosure, in
whole or in part, *
```

```
* of the IOSv Software or Documentation to any third
party for any        *
* purposes is expressly prohibited except as otherwise
authorized by       *
*              Cisco            in             writing.
*
********************************************************
****************
Switch>enable
Password:
Switch#conf t
Enter configuration commands, one per line.  End with
CNTL/Z.
Switch(config)#ip domain-name jaacostan.com
Switch(config)#crypto key generate rsa modulus 1024
The name for the keys will be: Switch.jaacostan.com

% The key modulus size is 1024 bits
% Generating 1024 bit RSA keys, keys will be non-
exportable...
[OK] (elapsed time was 0 seconds)

Switch(config)#
Switch(config)#line vty 0 4
Switch(config-line)#transport input ssh telnet
Switch(config-line)#end
Switch#write memory
Building configuration...
Compressed   configuration   from   3719   bytes   to   1730
bytes[OK]
Switch#exit

Configuring Switch 192.168.122.22

********************************************************
****************
*  IOSv  is  strictly  limited  to  use  for  evaluation,
demonstration and IOS  *
* education. IOSv is provided as-is and is not supported
by Cisco's       *
* Technical Advisory Center. Any use or disclosure, in
whole or in part, *
* of the IOSv Software or Documentation to any third
party for any        *
```

```
* purposes is expressly prohibited except as otherwise
authorized by     *
*            Cisco             in            writing.
*
*****************************************************
****************
Switch>enable
Password:
Switch#conf t
Enter configuration commands, one per line.   End with
CNTL/Z.
Switch(config)#ip domain-name jaacostan.com
Switch(config)#crypto key generate rsa modulus 1024
The name for the keys will be: Switch.jaacostan.com

% The key modulus size is 1024 bits
% Generating 1024 bit RSA keys, keys will be non-
exportable...
[OK] (elapsed time was 1 seconds)

Switch(config)#
Switch(config)#line vty 0 4
Switch(config-line)#transport input ssh telnet
Switch(config-line)#end
Switch#write memory
Building configuration...
Compressed  configuration  from  3719  bytes  to  1729
bytes[OK]
Switch#exit


Configuring Switch 192.168.122.23


*****************************************************
****************
*  IOSv  is  strictly  limited  to  use  for  evaluation,
demonstration and IOS  *
* education. IOSv is provided as-is and is not supported
by Cisco's     *
* Technical Advisory Center. Any use or disclosure, in
whole or in part, *
* of  the  IOSv  Software  or  Documentation  to  any  third
party for any     *
* purposes  is  expressly  prohibited  except  as  otherwise
authorized by     *
```

```
*           Cisco              in              writing.
*
* * * * * * * * * * * * * * * * * * * * * * * * * * * * * * * * * * * * * * * * * * * * * * * * * * * * *
* * * * * * * * * * * * * * * *
Switch>enable
Password:
Switch#conf t
Enter configuration commands, one per line.  End with
CNTL/Z.
Switch(config)#ip domain-name jaacostan.com
Switch(config)#crypto key generate rsa modulus 1024
The name for the keys will be: Switch.jaacostan.com

% The key modulus size is 1024 bits
% Generating 1024 bit RSA keys, keys will be non-
exportable...
[OK] (elapsed time was 0 seconds)

Switch(config)#
Switch(config)#line vty 0 4
Switch(config-line)#transport input ssh telnet
Switch(config-line)#end
Switch#write memory
Building configuration...
Compressed   configuration   from   3719   bytes   to   1728
bytes[OK]
Switch#exit

root@NetworkAutomation-PC:~#
```

So the code executed properly and successfully.
Now try to SSH in to the switch from your NetworkAutomation-PC.

Note: In some versions of the Automation appliance, you may encounter an error stating, Bad owner or permission.

```
root@NetworkAutomation-PC:~# ssh cisco@192.168.122.21
Bad owner or permissions on /root/.ssh/config
```

This error can be solved by changing permission.

```
root@NetworkAutomation-1:~#            cd            ..
root@NetworkAutomation-1:/#            cd            /etc
root@NetworkAutomation-1:/etc#        chown         root
/root/.ssh/config
```

```
root@NetworkAutomation-PC:/etc# cd ..
root@NetworkAutomation-PC:/# cd root

Now try ssh in to one of the switch,
root@NetworkAutomation-PC:~# ssh cisco@192.168.122.21
```

```
root@NetworkAutomation-PC:~# ls
ex1.py  ex1_a.py  ex2.py  ex3.py  ex4.py  ex5.py  ex6.py  switches.txt
root@NetworkAutomation-PC:~# ssh cisco@192.168.122.21
The authenticity of host '192.168.122.21 (192.168.122.21)' can't be established.
RSA key fingerprint is SHA256:t6YG3jJUQojjeVwqyMBtAP3iJpXgOGfOrR/ymYlC9Yc.
Are you sure you want to continue connecting (yes/no)? yes
Warning: Permanently added '192.168.122.21' (RSA) to the list of known hosts.

*****************************************************************
* IOSv is strictly limited to use for evaluation, demonstration and IOS  *
* education. IOSv is provided as-is and is not supported by Cisco's  *
* Technical Advisory Center. Any use or disclosure, in whole or in part,  *
* of the IOSv Software or Documentation to any third party for any  *
* purposes is expressly prohibited except as otherwise authorized by  *
* Cisco in writing.                                                  *
*****************************************************************Password:
```

```
root@NetworkAutomation-PC:~# ssh cisco@192.168.122.22
The authenticity of host '192.168.122.22 (192.168.122.22)' can't be established.
RSA key fingerprint is SHA256:7PE/NrUq2KJ2281OKa3FcRfKVATtI7olzZEn81+8UCw.
Are you sure you want to continue connecting (yes/no)? yes
Warning: Permanently added '192.168.122.22' (RSA) to the list of known hosts.

*****************************************************************
* IOSv is strictly limited to use for evaluation, demonstration and IOS  *
* education. IOSv is provided as-is and is not supported by Cisco's  *
* Technical Advisory Center. Any use or disclosure, in whole or in part,  *
* of the IOSv Software or Documentation to any third party for any  *
* purposes is expressly prohibited except as otherwise authorized by  *
* Cisco in writing.                                                  *
*****************************************************************Password:

*****************************************************************
* IOSv is strictly limited to use for evaluation, demonstration and IOS  *
* education. IOSv is provided as-is and is not supported by Cisco's  *
* Technical Advisory Center. Any use or disclosure, in whole or in part,  *
* of the IOSv Software or Documentation to any third party for any  *
* purposes is expressly prohibited except as otherwise authorized by  *
* Cisco in writing.                                                  *
*****************************************************************Switch>en
Password:
Switch#
```

Exercise 7: Backup the configuration of all switches.

In the real world, one of the task that administrators regularly do is taking the backup of device configuration.

Let's see how to automate this using python.

Code:

```
import getpass
import telnetlib

user = input("Enter your username :")
password = getpass.getpass()

f = open("switches.txt")
for IP in f:
```

<--- IP.strip() is used here to remove if any white-spaces contained in the IP addresses--->

```
    IP = IP.strip()
    print("Taking backup of Switch " + (IP))
    tn = telnetlib.Telnet(IP)
    tn.read_until(b"Username: ")
    tn.write(user.encode("ascii") + b"\n")
    if password:
        tn.read_until(b"Password: ")
        tn.write(password.encode("ascii") + b"\n")
    tn.write(b"enable\n")
    tn.write(b"cisco\n")
```

<--- terminal length 0 command eliminate the need to press enter key to show more configuration portion--->

```
    tn.write(b"terminal length 0\n")
    tn.write(b"show run\n")
    tn.write(b"exit\n")
```

<--- read all the output of the operations to a variable named as output--->

```
    output = tn.read_all()
```

<--- opening a file SW+IP address with write permission --->

```
config = open("SW" + IP, "w")
```

<--- write the configurations to the config variable, for each switch --->

```
    config.write(output.decode("ascii"))
```

```
config.write("\n")
```

<--- close the files opened --->

```
config.close
print(tn.read_all().decode("ascii"))
```

Once you created the python code, run it.
When successfully executed, you will get a similar output as shown as below.

```
root@NetworkAutomation-PC:~# python3 ex7.py
Enter your username :cisco
Password:
Taking backup of Switch 192.168.122.20

Taking backup of Switch 192.168.122.21

Taking backup of Switch 192.168.122.22

Taking backup of Switch 192.168.122.23

root@NetworkAutomation-PC:~# ^C
```

Now check your working directory whether the files are created or not.

```
root@NetworkAutomation-PC:~# ls -l
total 68
-rw-r--r-- 1 root root 4702 Sep 27 03:45 SW192.168.122.20
-rw-r--r-- 1 root root 4651 Sep 27 03:45 SW192.168.122.21
-rw-r--r-- 1 root root 4651 Sep 27 03:45 SW192.168.122.22
-rw-r--r-- 1 root root 4651 Sep 27 03:45 SW192.168.122.23
-rw-r--r-- 1 root root  511 Sep 26 17:49 ex1.py
-rw-r--r-- 1 root root  511 Sep 26 18:15 ex1_a.py
-rw-r--r-- 1 root root  468 Sep 26 18:27 ex2.py
-rw-r--r-- 1 root root  650 Sep 26 19:12 ex3.py
-rw-r--r-- 1 root root  642 Sep 26 22:20 ex4.py
-rw-r--r-- 1 root root  767 Sep 27 01:23 ex5.py
-rw-r--r-- 1 root root  791 Sep 27 03:02 ex6.py
-rw-r--r-- 1 root root  741 Sep 27 03:44 ex7.py
-rw-r--r-- 1 root root   60 Sep 26 23:34 switches.txt
root@NetworkAutomation-PC:~#
```

I can see the switch backup has been taken successfully.

Exercise 7: Summary

Code Summary

```
import getpass
```

```python
import telnetlib

user = input("Enter your username :")
password = getpass.getpass()

f = open("switches.txt")
for IP in f:
    IP = IP.strip()
    print("Taking backup of Switch " + (IP))
    tn = telnetlib.Telnet(IP)
    tn.read_until(b"Username: ")
    tn.write(user.encode("ascii") + b"\n")
    if password:
        tn.read_until(b"Password: ")
        tn.write(password.encode("ascii") + b"\n")
    tn.write(b"enable\n")
    tn.write(b"cisco\n")
    tn.write(b"terminal length 0\n")
    tn.write(b"show run\n")
    tn.write(b"exit\n")
    output = tn.read_all()
    config = open("SW" + IP, "w")
    config.write(output.decode("ascii"))
    config.write("\n")
    config.close
print(tn.read_all().decode("ascii"))
```

Executing the Code: Output

```
root@NetworkAutomation-PC:~# nano ex7.py
root@NetworkAutomation-PC:~# python3 ex7.py
Enter your username :cisco
Password:
Taking backup of Switch 192.168.122.20

Taking backup of Switch 192.168.122.21

Taking backup of Switch 192.168.122.22

Taking backup of Switch 192.168.122.23
```

```
root@NetworkAutomation-PC:~#
```

3.5 Netmiko Introduction.

So in all the previous exercises, we achieved our goals through telnet sessions. As we all know, telnet is not secure and may not be using in all environments. So we should be known to do all the automation tasks using SSH as well. Netmiko, developed by Kirk Byers is an open-source multivendor library that is used for SSH connections to network devices. Multi-vendor library means, Netmiko supports network devices from different vendors such as Cisco, Juniper , HP etc.

You may take a look at Netmiko documentation page at **https://github.com/ktbyers/netmiko**. We can perform configurations on network devices through SSH using the Netmiko.

Install the required packages and libraries, including Netmiko.

```
root@NetworkAutomation-PC:~# apt-get upgrade
root@NetworkAutomation-PC:~# apt-get install python3-pip
root@NetworkAutomation-PC:~# pip install --upgrade pip
root@NetworkAutomation-PC:~# pip install -U netmiko
```

In case the setup tools missing error you receive, then try the following commands.
```
#apt-get upgrade
#apt-get install python3-venv
#apt-get install python3-dev
#_pip install -U setuptools
#python3 -m  pip install --upgrade pip
#python3 -m  pip install setuptools
#python3 -m  pip install netmiko
```

When the operations are completed successfully, you can see similar messages.
```
Installing collected packages: pip
  Found existing installation: pip 9.0.3
    Uninstalling pip-9.0.3:
      Successfully uninstalled pip-9.0.3
Successfully installed pip-18.0
```

```
Installing collected packages: netmiko
  Found existing installation: netmiko 2.1.1
    Uninstalling netmiko-2.1.1:
      Successfully uninstalled netmiko-2.1.1
  Running setup.py install for netmiko ... done
Successfully installed netmiko-2.2.2
root@NetworkAutomation-PC:~#
```

If you are using a real device environment for this lab, then you may need to install the Netmiko on your Windows machine as well.

Installing Netmiko on linux is a matter of one single command but if you need to use Netmiko in your Windows PC, follow this process.

1) Install the latest version of Python.

2) Install Anaconda, which is an open source distribution platform that you can install in Windows and other OS's (**https://www.anaconda.com/download/**)

3) From the Anaconda Shell, run "**conda install paramiko**".

4) From the Anaconda Shell, run "**pip install scp**".

5) Now Install the Git for Windows.(**https://www.git-scm.com/downloads**).

Git is required for downloading and cloning all the Netmiko library files from Github.

6) From Git Bash window, Clone Netmiko using the following command

git clone https://github.com/ktbyers/netmiko&#8221

7) Once the installation is completed, change the directory to Netmiko **using cd netmiko** command.

8) Execute **python setup.py install** from Git Bash Window. Once the installation is completed, go to your Windows Command prompt or Anaconda shell and check Netmiko from Python Interpreter shell.

9) Finally **import paramiko** and **import netmiko**, and start using it for python coding.

In case you face any issue during installation, refer this link for installing Netmiko on Windows machine.
https://www.jaacostan.com/2018/09/how-to-install-netmiko-on-windows.html

Exercise 8: Create VLANs and Assign IP using SSH.

<--- importing netmiko package library for our code --->

```
from netmiko import ConnectHandler
```

<--- creating a dictionary for our perticular device, here the device is Cisco virtual IOS --->

```
iosv_12 = {
    'device_type': 'cisco_ios',
    'ip': '192.168.122.20',
    'username': 'cisco',
    'password': 'cisco',
    'secret' : 'cisco',
}
```

<--- calling the ConnectHandler Library [**iosv_12 means telling python to consider the contents of the dictionary as key value pairs instead of single elements. --->

```
net_connect = ConnectHandler(**iosv_12)
net_connect.enable()
```

<--- Sending a command in to the switch --->

```
output = net_connect.send_command("show ip int br")
print(output)
```

<--- Create a list that includes all the commands that we need to execute --->

```
config_commands = ['int vlan 5', 'ip add 5.5.5.1 255.255.255.0']
output = net_connect.send_config_set(config_commands)
print(output)

for n in range (10, 20):
    print("Creating VLAN " + str(n))
    config_commands = ['vlan ' + str(n), 'name DevOps_VLAN ' + str(n)]
    output = net_connect.send_config_set(config_commands)
    print(output)
```

After writing the code, execute it.You can see the output and then login to switch to verify the change

Exercise 8: Summary

Code Summary

```python
from netmiko import ConnectHandler

iosv_l2 = {
    'device_type': 'cisco_ios',
    'ip': '192.168.122.20',
    'username': 'cisco',
    'password': 'cisco',
    'secret' : 'cisco',
}

net_connect = ConnectHandler(**iosv_l2)
net_connect.enable()
output = net_connect.send_command("show ip int br")
print(output)

config_commands = ['int vlan 5', 'ip add 5.5.5.1
255.255.255.0']
output                                          =
net_connect.send_config_set(config_commands)
print(output)

for n in range (10, 20):
    print("Creating VLAN " + str(n))
    config_commands = ['vlan ' + str(n), 'name
DevOps_VLAN ' + str(n)]
    output                                      =
net_connect.send_config_set(config_commands)
    print(output)
```

```
from netmiko import ConnectHandler

iosv_12 = {
    'device_type': 'cisco_ios',
    'ip': '192.168.122.20',
    'username': 'cisco',
    'password': 'cisco',
    'secret' : 'cisco',
}

net_connect = ConnectHandler(**iosv_12)
net_connect.enable()
output = net_connect.send_command("show ip int br")
print(output)

config_commands = ['int vlan 5', 'ip add 5.5.5.1 255.255.255.0']
output = net_connect.send_config_set(config_commands)
print(output)

for n in range (10, 20):
    print("Creating VLAN " + str(n))
    config_commands = ['vlan ' + str(n), 'name DevOps_VLAN ' + str(n)]
    output = net_connect.send_config_set(config_commands)
    print(output)
```

Execute the Code: Output

```
root@NetworkAutomation-PC:~# python3 ex8.py
```

Interface	IP-Address	OK?	Method	Status	Protocol
GigabitEthernet0/0	unassigned	YES	unset	up	up
GigabitEthernet0/1	unassigned	YES	unset	up	up
GigabitEthernet0/2	unassigned	YES	unset	up	up
GigabitEthernet0/3	unassigned	YES	unset	up	up
GigabitEthernet1/0	unassigned	YES	unset	up	up
GigabitEthernet1/1	unassigned	YES	unset	up	up
GigabitEthernet1/2	unassigned	YES	unset	up	up
GigabitEthernet1/3	unassigned	YES	unset	up	up
GigabitEthernet2/0	unassigned	YES	unset	up	up

```
GigabitEthernet2/1      unassigned      YES unset  up
up
GigabitEthernet2/2      unassigned      YES unset  up
up
GigabitEthernet2/3      unassigned      YES unset  up
up
GigabitEthernet3/0      unassigned      YES unset  up
up
GigabitEthernet3/1      unassigned      YES unset  up
up
GigabitEthernet3/2      unassigned      YES unset  up
up
GigabitEthernet3/3      unassigned      YES unset  up
up
Vlan1                   192.168.122.20  YES NVRAM  up
up
Vlan5                   5.5.5.1             YES manual
administratively down down
Vlan20                  10.20.30.40         YES NVRAM
down                    down
config term
Enter  configuration  commands,  one  per  line.   End
with CNTL/Z.
CoreSW(config)#int vlan 5
CoreSW(config-if)#ip add 5.5.5.1 255.255.255.0
CoreSW(config-if)#end
CoreSW#
Creating VLAN 10
config term
Enter  configuration  commands,  one  per  line.   End
with CNTL/Z.
CoreSW(config)#vlan 10
CoreSW(config-vlan)#name DevOps_VLAN 10
CoreSW(config-vlan)#end
CoreSW#
Creating VLAN 11
config term
Enter  configuration  commands,  one  per  line.   End
with CNTL/Z.
CoreSW(config)#vlan 11
CoreSW(config-vlan)#name DevOps_VLAN 11
```

```
CoreSW(config-vlan)#end
CoreSW#
Creating VLAN 12
config term
Enter configuration commands, one per line.    End
with CNTL/Z.
CoreSW(config)#vlan 12
CoreSW(config-vlan)#name DevOps_VLAN 12
CoreSW(config-vlan)#end
CoreSW#
Creating VLAN 13
config term
Enter configuration commands, one per line.    End
with CNTL/Z.
CoreSW(config)#vlan 13
CoreSW(config-vlan)#name DevOps_VLAN 13
CoreSW(config-vlan)#end
CoreSW#
Creating VLAN 14
config term
Enter configuration commands, one per line.    End
with CNTL/Z.
CoreSW(config)#vlan 14
CoreSW(config-vlan)#name DevOps_VLAN 14
CoreSW(config-vlan)#end
CoreSW#
Creating VLAN 15
config term
Enter configuration commands, one per line.    End
with CNTL/Z.
CoreSW(config)#vlan 15
CoreSW(config-vlan)#name DevOps_VLAN 15
CoreSW(config-vlan)#end
CoreSW#
Creating VLAN 16
config term
Enter configuration commands, one per line.    End
with CNTL/Z.
CoreSW(config)#vlan 16
CoreSW(config-vlan)#name DevOps_VLAN 16
CoreSW(config-vlan)#end
```

```
CoreSW#
Creating VLAN 17
config term
Enter configuration commands, one per line.    End
with CNTL/Z.
CoreSW(config)#vlan 17
CoreSW(config-vlan)#name DevOps_VLAN 17
CoreSW(config-vlan)#end
CoreSW#
Creating VLAN 18
config term
Enter configuration commands, one per line.    End
with CNTL/Z.
CoreSW(config)#vlan 18
CoreSW(config-vlan)#name DevOps_VLAN 18
CoreSW(config-vlan)#end
CoreSW#
Creating VLAN 19
config term
Enter configuration commands, one per line.    End
with CNTL/Z.
CoreSW(config)#vlan 19
CoreSW(config-vlan)#name DevOps_VLAN 19
CoreSW(config-vlan)#end
CoreSW#
root@NetworkAutomation-PC:~#
```

Exercise 9: Create Multiple VLANs on all switches using SSH.

In this exercise, we are going to create 5 additional VLANs on all our remaining 3 Switches (SW1, SW2, SW3). In the code, we are using nested for loops.

```
from netmiko import ConnectHandler

switch1 = {
    'device_type': 'cisco_ios',
    'ip': '192.168.122.21',
    'username': 'cisco',
    'password': 'cisco',
    'secret' : 'cisco',
}

switch2 = {
    'device_type': 'cisco_ios',
    'ip': '192.168.122.22',
    'username': 'cisco',
    'password': 'cisco',
    'secret' : 'cisco',
}

switch3 = {
    'device_type': 'cisco_ios',
    'ip': '192.168.122.23',
    'username': 'cisco',
    'password': 'cisco',
    'secret' : 'cisco',
}

switches = [switch1, switch2, switch3]

for devices in switches:
    net_connect = ConnectHandler(**devices)
    net_connect.enable()
    for n in range (10, 15):
        print("Creating VLAN " + str(n))
        config_commands = ['vlan ' + str(n), 'name DevOps_VLAN ' + str(n)]
        output = net_connect.send_config_set(config_commands)
        print(output)
```

Exercise 9: Summary

Code Summary

```
from netmiko import ConnectHandler

switch1 = {
    'device_type': 'cisco_ios',
    'ip': '192.168.122.21',
    'username': 'cisco',
    'password': 'cisco',
    'secret' : 'cisco',
}

switch2 = {
    'device_type': 'cisco_ios',
    'ip': '192.168.122.22',
```

```
    'username': 'cisco',
    'password': 'cisco',
    'secret' : 'cisco',
}

switch3 = {
    'device_type': 'cisco_ios',
    'ip': '192.168.122.23',
    'username': 'cisco',
    'password': 'cisco',
    'secret' : 'cisco',
}

switches = [switch1, switch2, switch3]

for devices in switches:
    net_connect = ConnectHandler(**devices)
    net_connect.enable()
    for n in range (10, 15):
        print("Creating VLAN " + str(n))
        config_commands = ['vlan ' + str(n), 'name DevOps_VLAN
' + str(n)]
        output = net_connect.send_config_set(config_commands)
        print(output)
```

Execute Code: Output

```
root@NetworkAutomation-PC:~# python3 ex9.py
Creating VLAN 10
config term
Enter configuration commands, one per line.  End with CNTL/Z.
SW1(config)#vlan 10
SW1(config-vlan)#name DevOps_VLAN 10
SW1(config-vlan)#end
SW1#
Creating VLAN 11
config term
Enter configuration commands, one per line.  End with CNTL/Z.
SW1(config)#vlan 11
SW1(config-vlan)#name DevOps_VLAN 11
SW1(config-vlan)#end
SW1#
Creating VLAN 12
config term
Enter configuration commands, one per line.  End with CNTL/Z.
SW1(config)#vlan 12
SW1(config-vlan)#name DevOps_VLAN 12
SW1(config-vlan)#end
SW1#
Creating VLAN 13
```

```
config term
Enter configuration commands, one per line.  End with CNTL/Z.
SW1(config)#vlan 13
SW1(config-vlan)#name DevOps_VLAN 13
SW1(config-vlan)#end
SW1#
Creating VLAN 14
config term
Enter configuration commands, one per line.  End with CNTL/Z.
SW1(config)#vlan 14
SW1(config-vlan)#name DevOps_VLAN 14
SW1(config-vlan)#end
SW1#
Creating VLAN 10
config term
Enter configuration commands, one per line.  End with CNTL/Z.
SW2(config)#vlan 10
SW2(config-vlan)#name DevOps_VLAN 10
SW2(config-vlan)#end
SW2#
Creating VLAN 11
config term
Enter configuration commands, one per line.  End with CNTL/Z.
SW2(config)#vlan 11
SW2(config-vlan)#name DevOps_VLAN 11
SW2(config-vlan)#end
SW2#
Creating VLAN 12
config term
Enter configuration commands, one per line.  End with CNTL/Z.
SW2(config)#vlan 12
SW2(config-vlan)#name DevOps_VLAN 12
SW2(config-vlan)#end
SW2#
Creating VLAN 13
config term
Enter configuration commands, one per line.  End with CNTL/Z.
SW2(config)#vlan 13
SW2(config-vlan)#name DevOps_VLAN 13
SW2(config-vlan)#end
SW2#
Creating VLAN 14
config term
Enter configuration commands, one per line.  End with CNTL/Z.
SW2(config)#vlan 14
SW2(config-vlan)#name DevOps_VLAN 14
SW2(config-vlan)#end
SW2#
Creating VLAN 10
```

```
config term
Enter configuration commands, one per line.  End with CNTL/Z.
SW3(config)#vlan 10
SW3(config-vlan)#name DevOps_VLAN 10
SW3(config-vlan)#end
SW3#
Creating VLAN 11
config term
Enter configuration commands, one per line.  End with CNTL/Z.
SW3(config)#vlan 11
SW3(config-vlan)#name DevOps_VLAN 11
SW3(config-vlan)#end
SW3#
Creating VLAN 12
config term
Enter configuration commands, one per line.  End with CNTL/Z.
SW3(config)#vlan 12
SW3(config-vlan)#name DevOps_VLAN 12
SW3(config-vlan)#end
SW3#
Creating VLAN 13
config term
Enter configuration commands, one per line.  End with CNTL/Z.
SW3(config)#vlan 13
SW3(config-vlan)#name DevOps_VLAN 13
SW3(config-vlan)#end
SW3#
Creating VLAN 14
config term
Enter configuration commands, one per line.  End with CNTL/Z.
SW3(config)#vlan 14
SW3(config-vlan)#name DevOps_VLAN 14
SW3(config-vlan)#end
SW3#
```

Exercise 10: Upload the configurations on all switches using SSH.

In this exercise, our goal is to achieve the following configurations. Also instead of specifying the cisco commands in your python code, we will create a text file and put all the required commands in that. Then later, call the text file that has all the commands, in to the python code.

This kind of situations may me encountered often during network operations. The architect or senior engineer may distribute the configuration commands to the administrator and the administrator just need to execute the commands in each switches. Manually doing this task is a time consuming one.

With python coding, we can achieve this goal in seconds.

So we need to do the following changes to all the three switches.

1) Create a new user
2) Assign an NTP server
3) Enable 4 ports and assign them an access VLAN.
4) Save the configurations.

For doing this, first I created a file named as config_change.txt in nano editor with all the required commands.

Once you created the file, use cat command to view the contents.

```
root@NetworkAutomation-PC:~# cat config_change.txt
username jaa password jaa
ntp server 1.2.3.4
int range gig 3/0 - 3
 switchport access vlan 10
 switchport mode access
 no sh
end
wri mem
```

Now write the code.

```python
from netmiko import ConnectHandler

switch1 = {
    'device_type': 'cisco_ios',
    'ip': '192.168.122.21',
    'username': 'cisco',
    'password': 'cisco',
    'secret' : 'cisco',
}

switch2 = {
    'device_type': 'cisco_ios',
    'ip': '192.168.122.22',
    'username': 'cisco',
    'password': 'cisco',
    'secret' : 'cisco',
}

switch3 = {
    'device_type': 'cisco_ios',
    'ip': '192.168.122.23',
    'username': 'cisco',
    'password': 'cisco',
```

```
    'secret' : 'cisco',
}

switches = [switch1, switch2, switch3]
```

<--- Open the config_change.txt file that has all the commands that we need to execute and read lines --->

```
with open('config_change.txt') as f:
    lines = f.read().splitlines()
print(lines)

for devices in switches:
    net_connect = ConnectHandler(**devices)
    net_connect.enable()
```

<--- Call each command line by line and send to the switch --->

```
    output = net_connect.send_config_set(lines)
    print(output))
```

Exercise 10: Summary

Config_change.txt file

```
root@NetworkAutomation-PC:~# cat config_change.txt
username jaa password jaa
ntp server 1.2.3.4
int range gig 3/0 - 3
 switchport access vlan 10
 switchport mode access
 no sh
end
wri mem
```

Code Summary

```
from netmiko import ConnectHandler

switch1 = {
    'device_type': 'cisco_ios',
    'ip': '192.168.122.21',
    'username': 'cisco',
    'password': 'cisco',
    'secret' : 'cisco',
```

```
}

switch2 = {
    'device_type': 'cisco_ios',
    'ip': '192.168.122.22',
    'username': 'cisco',
    'password': 'cisco',
    'secret' : 'cisco',
}

switch3 = {
    'device_type': 'cisco_ios',
    'ip': '192.168.122.23',
    'username': 'cisco',
    'password': 'cisco',
    'secret' : 'cisco',
}

switches = [switch1, switch2, switch3]

with open('config_change.txt') as f:
    lines = f.read().splitlines()
print(lines)

for devices in switches:
    net_connect = ConnectHandler(**devices)
    net_connect.enable()
    output = net_connect.send_config_set(lines)
    print(output)
```

Code output

```
root@NetworkAutomation-PC:~# python3 ex10.py
['username jaa password jaa', 'ntp server 1.2.3.4', 'int
range gig 3/0 - 3', ' switchport access vlan 10', '
switchport mode access', ' no sh', 'end', 'wri mem', '']
config term
Enter configuration commands, one per line.  End with
CNTL/Z.
SW1(config)#username jaa password jaa
SW1(config)#ntp server 1.2.3.4
SW1(config)#int range gig 3/0 - 3
SW1(config-if-range)# switchport access vlan 10
SW1(config-if-range)# switchport mode access
SW1(config-if-range)# no sh
```

```
SW1(config-if-range)#end
SW1#wri mem
Building configuration...

config term
Enter configuration commands, one per line.  End with
CNTL/Z.
SW2(config)#username jaa password jaa
SW2(config)#ntp server 1.2.3.4
SW2(config)#int range gig 3/0 - 3
SW2(config-if-range)# switchport access vlan 10
SW2(config-if-range)# switchport mode access
SW2(config-if-range)# no sh
SW2(config-if-range)#end
SW2#wri mem
Building configuration...

config term
Enter configuration commands, one per line.  End with
CNTL/Z.
SW3(config)#username jaa password jaa
SW3(config)#ntp server 1.2.3.4
SW3(config)#int range gig 3/0 - 3
SW3(config-if-range)# switchport access vlan 10
SW3(config-if-range)# switchport mode access
SW3(config-if-range)# no sh
SW3(config-if-range)#end
SW3#wri mem
Building configuration...

root@NetworkAutomation-PC:~#
root@NetworkAutomation-PC:~# cat config_change.txt
username jaa password jaa
ntp server 1.2.3.4
int range gig 3/0 - 3
 switchport access vlan 10
 switchport mode access
 no sh
end
wri mem
```

Exercise 11: Apply different configuration to different switches.

In this exercise, we will be getting familiarize with the concept of how to apply different configuration to different switch using a single python code.

Goal:

1) Remove the VLANs 11 to 15 from all the switches.
2) And configure a new VLAN_25 interface (SVI) only on Switch3(SW3) and assign it on gig2/0.

So first we need to create a configuration file for all the switches. Then we need to create another configuration file exclusively for Switch3. Call these files separately in the python code and that is how we can bale to achieve our goal.

Exercise 11: Summary

all_switches.txt

```
no vlan 11
no vlan 12
no vlan 13
no vlan 14
no vlan 15
exit
write mem
```

Switch_3.txt

```
vlan 25
name Python_VLAN_25
exit
int vlan 25
ip add 25.25.25.1 255.255.255.0
no sh
end
write mem
```

Code:
```
from netmiko import ConnectHandler

switch1 = {
```

```
    'device_type': 'cisco_ios',
    'ip': '192.168.122.21',
    'username': 'cisco',
    'password': 'cisco',
    'secret' : 'cisco',
}

switch2 = {
    'device_type': 'cisco_ios',
    'ip': '192.168.122.22',
    'username': 'cisco',
    'password': 'cisco',
    'secret' : 'cisco',
}

switch3 = {
    'device_type': 'cisco_ios',
    'ip': '192.168.122.23',
    'username': 'cisco',
    'password': 'cisco',
    'secret' : 'cisco',
}

switches = [switch1, switch2, switch3]

with open('all_switches.txt') as f:
    lines = f.read().splitlines()
print(lines)

for devices in switches:
    net_connect = ConnectHandler(**devices)
    net_connect.enable()
    output = net_connect.send_config_set(lines)
    print(output)

with open('switch_3.txt') as f:
    lines = f.read().splitlines()
print(lines)

net_connect = ConnectHandler(**switch3)
net_connect.enable()
output = net_connect.send_config_set(lines)
print(output)
```

Code Output

```
root@NetworkAutomation-PC:~# python3 ex11.py
['no vlan 11', 'no vlan 12', 'no vlan 13', 'no vlan 14',
'no vlan 15', 'exit', 'write mem', '', '']
config term
Enter configuration commands, one per line.    End with
CNTL/Z.
SW1(config)#no vlan 11
SW1(config)#no vlan 12
SW1(config)#no vlan 13
SW1(config)#no vlan 14
SW1(config)#no vlan 15
SW1(config)#exit
SW1#write mem
Building configuration...

config term
Enter configuration commands, one per line.    End with
CNTL/Z.
SW2(config)#no vlan 11
SW2(config)#no vlan 12
SW2(config)#no vlan 13
SW2(config)#no vlan 14
SW2(config)#no vlan 15
SW2(config)#exit
SW2#write mem
Building configuration...

config term
Enter configuration commands, one per line.    End with
CNTL/Z.
SW3(config)#no vlan 11
SW3(config)#no vlan 12
SW3(config)#no vlan 13
SW3(config)#no vlan 14
SW3(config)#no vlan 15
SW3(config)#exit
SW3#write mem
Building configuration...

['vlan 25', 'name Python_VLAN_25', 'exit', 'int vlan 25',
'ip add 25.25.25.1 255.255.255.0', 'no sh', 'end', 'write
mem']
config term
```

```
Enter  configuration  commands,  one  per  line.   End  with
CNTL/Z.
SW3(config)#vlan 25
SW3(config-vlan)#name Python_VLAN_25
SW3(config-vlan)#exit
SW3(config)#int vlan 25
SW3(config-if)#ip add 25.25.25.1 255.255.255.0
SW3(config-if)#no sh
SW3(config-if)#end
SW3#write mem
Building configuration...
```

Verify Switch 3:

```
SW3#show run int vlan25
Building configuration...

Current configuration : 61 bytes
!
interface Vlan25
 ip address 25.25.25.1 255.255.255.0
end
```

```
VLAN Name                             Status    Ports
---- -------------------------------- --------- -------------------------------
1    default                          active    Gi0/0, Gi0/1, Gi0/2, Gi0/3
                                                Gi1/0, Gi1/1, Gi1/2, Gi1/3
                                                Gi2/0, Gi2/1, Gi2/2, Gi2/3
2    Data_VLAN_2                       active
3    Data_VLAN_3                       active
4    Data_VLAN_4                       active
5    Data_VLAN_5                       active
6    Data_VLAN_6                       active
7    Data_VLAN_7                       active
8    Data_VLAN_8                       active
9    Data_VLAN_9                       active
10   DevOps_VLAN 10                    active    Gi3/0, Gi3/1, Gi3/2, Gi3/3
16   DevOps_VLAN 16                    active
17   DevOps_VLAN 17                    active
18   DevOps_VLAN 18                    active
19   DevOps_VLAN 19                    active
25   Python_VLAN_25                    active
1002 fddi-default                     act/unsup
1003 token-ring-default               act/unsup
1004 fddinet-default                  act/unsup
1005 trnet-default                    act/unsup
SW3#
```

Summary

So that is it. In this book I have covered the basics of python programming which includes the various data types, strings and numbers, lists and dictionaries, conditions, loops as well as python functions with clear examples that are vital for coding network automation.

Then I illustrated how to setup the lab environment for network automation using GNS3. There were 11 exercises to practice the real-world scenarios. I also provided an introduction on Netmiko and shown how to make use of Netmiko to automate the network tasks over SSH.

This book is intended mainly for Network administrators who are in to operations and service delivery. This books makes the Network engineer to get familiarize with the python3 programming and helps them to compete in the challenging career environment.

Once again, I urge all the readers to practice the codes multiple times regularly.

Also encourages you to tweak the codes or write new codes to achieve new goals and for new configurations.

All the diagrams, IP addresses, numbers, names etc. used in this book is only for illustration purposes. They doesn't represent anything other than for examples and illustration. All the proprietary terms, reference links used here belongs to the respective owners.

I hope this book was informative to you and I wish all the best to you.

Note:

If you liked this book, please leave a review in the Amazon website.

Take a look in to my Amazon author profile to view all by books.

amazon.com/author/jithinalex

BEING A FIREWALL ENGINEER: AN OPERATIONAL APPROACH:

A Comprehensive guide on firewall management operations and best practices

Understand different firewall products and the Packet-flows. Hardening and best practices of firewall management with real world example. Get familiarize with Change management and understand how to incorporate change management process in to firewall management operations.

This book give you a broad overview on Firewalls, packet flows, hardening, management & operations and the best practices followed in the industry. Though this book is mainly intended for firewall administrators who are in to operations, this book give a quick introduction and comparisons of the major firewall vendors and their products.

In this book I have covered the following topics.
•Various Job roles related to Firewalls.
•What makes you a firewall expert?
•Know the major firewall vendors and their models.
•Understand the packet flow or order of operation in each firewall.
•Understand the different types of firewalls.
•Understand the daily tasks of a firewall administrator
•Understand device hardening.
•Guidelines on hardening the firewalls.
•Explains major hardening standards and compliance.
•Understand Change Management process.
•Illustration on How to make a firewall change (incorporating Change management process) with a real world example.

Cisco Firepower Threat Defense (FTD) NGFW: An Administrator's Handbook: A 100% practical guide on configuring and managing Cisco FTD using Cisco FMC and FDM.

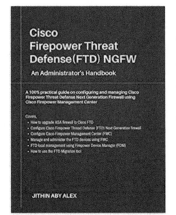

This book is written like a learning course, explained in detail with a lab topology using FTDv and FMCv. Hence this is a 100% practical guide on configuring and managing Cisco Firepower Threat Defense Next Generation Firewall using Cisco Firepower Management Center.

Covers,
•How to upgrade ASA firewall to Cisco FTD (Migration and Upgrade)
•Configure Cisco Firepower Threat Defense (FTD) Next Generation firewall
•Configure Cisco Firepower Management Center (FMC)
•Manage and administer the FTD devices using FMC (Configure interfaces, zones, routing, ACLs, Prefilter policies, NAT, High Availability etc)
•FTD local management using Firepower Device Manager (FDM)
•Introduction to the FTD Migration tool

Security Incident Handling: A Comprehensive Guide on Incident Handling and Response

Covers,

- Security Incident Handling Framework
- Types of threats and its countermeasures
- Building an effective security incident handling policy and team
- Prepare a Security Incident Report

This book has four major sections, The first section gives an introduction on Security incident Handling and response frameworks. Also give a glimpse on Security forensics and Risk Management concepts.

The second section explains different kinds of security threats and attacks that can result in potential security incident. Being familiarize with the attacks are very important for identifying and categorizing a security incident. The third section mentions the security controls and countermeasures to detect, prevent or/and to mitigate a threat. This includes the detection mechanisms, defense in depth, vulnerability management etc. The strategy and plan for building an efficient Security Incident Handing is comprehensively explained in the final section. The six phases of a security incident handling and response are explained step by step.

www.ingramcontent.com/pod-product-compliance
Lightning Source LLC
LaVergne TN
LVHW081531050326
832903LV00025B/1729